How to use E

In this issue

The 92 daily readings in this issue of *Explore* are designed to help you understand and apply the Bible as you read it each day.

It's serious!

We suggest that you allow 15 minutes each day to work through the Bible passage with the notes. It should be a meal, not a snack! Readings from other parts of the Bible can throw valuable light on the study passage. These cross-references can be skipped if you are already feeling full up, but will expand your grasp of the Bible. *Explore* uses the NIV2011 Bible translation, but you can also use it with the NIV1984 or ESV translations.

Sometimes a prayer section will encourage you to stop and pray through the lessons—but it is always important to allow time to pray for God's Spirit to bring his word to life, and to shape the way we think and live through it.

We're serious!

All of us who work on Explore share a passion for getting the Bible into people's lives. We fiercely hold to the Bible as God's word— to honour and follow, not to explain away.

1 Find a time you can read the Bible each day

2 Find a place where you can be quiet and think

3 Ask God to help you understand

4 Carefully read through the Bible passage for today

5 Study the verses with Explore, taking time to think

6 Pray about what you have read

thegoodbook COMPANY

Opening up the Bible

Welcome

Tim Thornborough is the Publishing Director at The Good Book Company

Being a Christian isn't a skill you learn, like carpentry or flower arranging. Nor is it a lifestyle choice, like the kind of clothes you wear, or the people you choose to hang out with. It's about having a real relationship with the living God through his Son, Jesus Christ. The Bible tells us that this relationship is like a marriage.

It's important to start with this, because many Christians view the practice of daily Bible reading as a Christian duty, or a hard discipline that is just one more thing to get done in our busy modern lives.

But the Bible is God speaking to us: opening his mind to us on how he thinks, what he wants for us and what his plans are for the world. And most importantly, it tells us what he has done for us in sending his Son, Jesus Christ, into the world. It's the way that the Spirit shows Jesus to us, and changes us as we behold his glory.

The Bible is not a manual. It's a love letter. And as with any love letter, we'll want to treasure it, and make time to read and re-read it, so we know we are loved, and discover how we can please the One who loves us. Here are a few suggestions for making your daily time with God more of a joy than a burden:

- *Time:* Find a time when you will not be disturbed, and when the cobwebs are cleared from your mind. Many people have found that the morning is the best time as it sets you up for the day. If you're not a "morning person", then last thing at night or a mid-morning break may suit you. Whatever works for you is right for you.

- *Place:* Jesus says that we are not to make a great show of our religion *(see Matthew 6:5-6)*, but rather, to pray with the door to our room shut. Some people plan to get to work a few minutes earlier and get their Bible out in an office or some other quiet corner.

- *Prayer:* Although *Explore* helps with specific prayer ideas from the passage, you should try to develop your own lists to pray through. Use the flap inside the back cover to help with this. And allow what you read in the Scriptures to shape what you pray for yourself, the world and others.

- *Share:* As the saying goes: *expression deepens impression*. So try to cultivate the habit of sharing with others what you have learned. Why not join our Facebook group to share your encouragements, questions and prayer requests? Search for *Explore: For your daily walk with God.*

And remember, *it's quality, not quantity, that counts:* better to think briefly about a single verse than to skim through pages without absorbing anything, because it's about developing your relationship with the living God. The sign that your daily time with God is real is when you start to love him more and serve him more wholeheartedly.

tim

HABAKKUK: How long?

If you've ever looked at evil and suffering and wondered "Why doesn't God do something about it?" you're not alone. Habakkuk was asking the same question 2600 years ago.

How long?

Habakkuk was writing at the close of the 7th century BC in Judah, the southern kingdom of God's people.

Read Habakkuk 1:1-4

- ❓ *What caused Habakkuk to ask God "How long?" and "Why?"?*
- ❓ *What picture does he paint of life among God's people in Judah at the time?*

Be amazed!

Read Habakkuk 1:5-11

Habakkuk was frustrated that God wasn't doing anything about the sins of the people. In verse 5 God reveals that he is going to act.

- ❓ *What impact would this revelation of God's work have on Habakkuk and the people (v 5)?*
- ❓ *What was God going to do (v 6)?*
- ❓ *Why was this so unbelievable?*

Verses 6-11 describe the invaders.

- ❓ *What do we learn about the Babylonians —what they were like, and how they treated their enemies?*

···· **TIME OUT** ·····································

The Babylonian siege of Jerusalem lasted two years.

- ❓ *What do the following verses reveal about the suffering in the city during this time? Lamentations 4:4, 8, 10; 5:11-12.*

⌄ Apply

Even though the Babylonians committed these atrocities, ultimately this was God's work of judgment.

- ❓ *What does it tell us about God's holiness and attitude to sin?*
- ❓ *How does this challenge your view of what God is like?*

In the death of Jesus on the cross, we see God judging the sins of his people again.

- ❓ *What is the same as this Old Testament judgment? What is different?*
- ❓ *Why should we "be utterly amazed" even more at this judgment on sin?*
- ❓ *What is the warning in Acts 13:40-41 if we don't believe in what Jesus has done?*

Jesus took the judgment our sins deserve, but we should be ruthless in putting our sins to death (Colossians 3:5; Romans 8:13).

- ❓ *How should what we've seen in Habakkuk (about God's holiness and hatred of sin) help us respond this way?*

⌃ Pray

Give thanks that Jesus has endured the terrible judgment we deserve. Pray that you would be ruthless in putting sin to death.

The wicked prosper

Kim Jong-un, the North Korean leader, lives a life of self-indulgent luxury—private jet, £6m yacht, 17 palaces, 100 cars—while his oppressed people struggle for survival.

❓ *Why does God allow it?*

Habakkuk was struggling with the same issue of why God allows the wicked to prosper. His first question to God in 1:2-4 was about why God didn't do anything about the wicked in Judah. God responded (v 5-11) that he was going to raise up the Babylonians to inflict terrible judgment on Judah. But that just provoked another question.

The character of God

Read Habakkuk 1:12 – 2:1

❓ *What aspects of God's character does Habakkuk highlight (1 v 12-13)?*

⌄ Apply

As Habakkuk puzzled over what was going on, he reminded himself (and God) of what God is like. And that is a good model for us. Remembering God's unchanging character gives us a rock to stand on in the storm.

⌃ Pray

Take a moment to thank the Lord for what he is like, using phrases from verses 12-13.

The wicked prosper

Habakkuk didn't actually doubt God's character. What puzzled him was why God was going to act in the way he said, given what he is like.

❓ *What was Habakkuk's question (v 13)?*
❓ *In what ways were the wicked Babylonians prospering (v 14-17)?*
❓ *A fishing image runs through these verses. How does it emphasise both the success and the wickedness of the Babylonians?*

The Babylonians, with their false gods, ruthless aggression, and expanding empire, were having a great time of it. Under King Nebuchadnezzar the capital, Babylon, became the jewel in the crown of the empire. Its hanging gardens were one of the wonders of the ancient world.

···· TIME OUT ····

Read Psalm 73

❓ *How is it similar to this passage?*

It didn't seem right then, and it doesn't seem right today, that the wicked prosper. But we need to do what Habakkuk did.

❓ *What did he resolve to do (Habakkuk 2:1)?*
❓ *How was he like a man on sentry duty?*

God's response is the rest of chapter 2.

⌃ Pray

Pray that the prosperity of the wicked would not make you despair, give up, or turn against God. Pray that instead you will look to him and keep trusting.

Wait for it…

Why God allows the wicked to prosper is something that puzzled Habakkuk and may well puzzle us today. God's answer requires us to wait and to trust.

…wait for it…

Read Habakkuk 2:2-5

God's answer to Habakkuk's question (1:12-17) was "the revelation" of coming judgment in chapter 2. Habakkuk was to write it on tablets (v 2)—of clay or wood—so that it could be preserved and passed on to others. "Run" (v 2) is a term used of the prophets passing their message on (Jeremiah 23:21).

> ❷ *What three things do these verses in Habakkuk tell us about when the vision would be fulfilled?*
> ❷ *And what three things about how certain it is?*
> ❷ *And what one thing about how we should respond to it?*

Although the utterly vile Babylonians were prospering, God's judgment on them was coming. But Habakkuk needed to be patient and wait for it.

✓ Apply

The time would come for Babylon, and will come for our world today. But it is God's appointed time not ours. We're used to watching films in which everything is resolved in the space of two hours. But God is "from everlasting" (1:12) and is working on a different timescale.

> ❷ *What is the encouragement to us in 2 Peter 3:8-9 as we wait? And what is the challenge in Hebrews 10:36-39?*

Trust in him

Read Habakkuk 2:2-5 again

Verses 4-5 contrast two groups of people—the wicked and the righteous.

> ❷ *How are the wicked described?*
> ❷ *What is the hallmark of the righteous?*

In contrast to the wicked Babylonians and the wicked in Judah, there was a righteous remnant who trusted in the Lord. And there still is today.

Verse 4 is quoted three times in the New Testament (Romans 1:17; Galatians 3:11; Hebrews 10:38).

> ❷ *What does it mean?*
> ❷ *Why has it become such a key verse?*

···· TIME OUT ····

Many of the "righteous by faith" did survive the Babylonian invasion, because they surrendered as the prophets told them to (Jeremiah 21:8-9) and were taken into exile in Babylon. And then some of them returned to Judah 70 years later.

⌃ Pray

Give thanks that by faith in Christ we are declared righteous in God's sight, and will escape the coming judgment.

Pray for those people you know who don't yet enjoy that assurance.

Worship and warning

In Psalm 95 we hear a voice exhorting the people of God to join in enthusiastic songs of worship (v 1-7a)—and also to listen to God's voice and heed his warning (v 7b-11).

Read Psalm 95:1-7a

- ❓ *What does the psalmist exhort us to do in verses 1-2?*
- ❓ *What does this celebration sound like?*
- ❓ *Why would we want to join this noisy exuberance (v 3-5)?*
- ❓ *How do verses 6-7 contrast with 3-5?*
- ❓ *What phrases show that there is no one greater than God (v 1-7)?*

The voice of this leader of the people of God exhorts us to join a noisy celebration because there is one true God, and only one, who is the unrivalled Creator of all things. In verse 6, alongside the jubilant enthusiasm, there is a deeply humble bowing down. The words "bow down", "worship" and "kneel" have this in common: the movement is vertical and always downwards! This kind of shared singing moves our hearts and bodies to a willing submission to the God whom we praise.

⌄ Apply

The God whom we worship when we sing and bow down corporately in church is the God who made and shaped and controls the whole world. This gives to our corporate worship a sense both of gladness (v 1-2) and deep reverence (v 6).

- ❓ *How can you hold together both an exultant gladness and a deep humility when a) you worship with your church family, and b) you worship alone?*

Read Psalm 95:7b-11

- ❓ *What does God tell his people NOT to do, and why?*
- ❓ *It's tempting to enjoy verses 1-7a, but ignore verses 7b-11. Why must we not do this?*

In verse 8 the psalmist says, effectively, *Think back to that place that came to be nicknamed "Strife" (Meribah) and what happened there (Exodus 17:1-7). Think back to that later place that we called "Testing" (Massah) and what happened there (Numbers 20:1-13).* In those places the people of God hardened their hearts against God.

These verses are quoted in Hebrews 3 and 4, where it's clear that the faith we are called to is specifically faith in the Lord Jesus Christ. *This* is how we will enter God's rest.

The placing of Psalm 95:1-7a and 7b-11 teaches us something of enduring importance. True worship, expressed corporately in joyful song and humble prayer, is marked by an eager attentiveness to the word of God and a careful obedience to that word from the heart. Let us be very careful to hear and to heed all eleven verses of this psalm!

⌃ Pray

- ❓ *Which do you find hardest: the call to joyful celebration, or to careful obedience?*

Ask God to help you do both.

Bible in a year: Ezekiel 35-36 • John 17

The sins God judges

When a sexual abuser is jailed, a dictator toppled, or a war criminal convicted, then people cheer. But when they get away with it, people groan. We want justice. And God assures us that justice is coming.

Habakkuk was perplexed that God would use the wicked Babylonians to judge his people. But God revealed that one day the Babylonians would be called to account. On that day the nations they had conquered would mock them (v 6). Their taunts are structured around five "woes", describing the sins of the Babylonians and the judgment that would come on them—and those like them.

Read Habakkuk 2:6-20

Plundering

❓ *What's the sin and judgment? (v 6-8)?*
❓ *To plunder means to take what is not yours, either by violence or dishonesty. What are examples of this today?*

Exploitation

❓ *What's the sin and judgment? (v 9-11)?*
❓ *How are tobacco, illegal drugs and gambling examples of people building their houses through "unjust gain"?*

Empire building

❓ *What's the sin and judgment (v 12-14)?*

What was true of Babylon is true of any empire built on sin. In judgment they will one day fall.

Abuse

❓ *What's the sin and judgment (v 15-17)?*

❓ *Where might we see a modern example of this?*

Idolatry

❓ *What is the sin (v 18-20)?*
❓ *Why is idolatry sheer folly?*
❓ *What are examples of idolatry in our world today?*

The judgment of God

This prophecy against Babylon was fulfilled in 539 BC when God raised up the Persians under King Cyrus to destroy them. God is sovereignly at work to judge in history, raising up one nation or empire to bring down another. And then in turn judging them. But Babylon reappears in Revelation chapter 18 as a picture of a world in rebellion against God and heading for final judgment. Revelation 18:4 says "Come out of her, my people".

❓ *What does it mean to "come out of Babylon"?*
❓ *What does it not mean?*

🔼 Pray

Give thanks that as the "righteous live through faith" we know that Jesus has drunk for us the cup of judgment we deserve. Pray that you will be in the world, but not of the world—turning from worldliness and living righteously.

Bible in a year: Ezekiel 37-39 • John 18:1-18

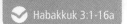
Ready or not, here I come!

God had revealed to Habakkuk that he would come in judgment—on Judah and, in time, on Babylon. Chapter 3 is the prophet's response.

Believe in God's coming

Read Habakkuk 3:1-2

Habakkuk had heard and read of God coming in judgment in the past.

> ❷ *What was his response to this?*
> ❷ *And what did he pray as he looked to the future?*

We can now look back on God coming in history in judgment on the sins of his people on the cross, bringing salvation.

⌃ Pray

Give thanks for the cross, where God in wrath remembered mercy. And give thanks that this coming of Christ assures us he will also return as promised, to deal with evil once and for all, and to save his people.

Tremble at his coming

What follows is a description of God coming in judgment. It's put in the past tense, but is looking to the future.

Read Habakkuk 3:3-7

> ❷ *What details emphasise God's splendour and glory?*
> ❷ *What effect does his coming have on the natural world, and on the enemies of his people?*

Centuries after Habakkuk, when God came in Christ, the surprise was that his glory and power were largely veiled, although at times revealed to his witnesses. But when he returns it will be in awesome power and glory, as described here.

Read Habakkuk 3:8-16a

> ❷ *What details picture God as a victorious warrior?*
> ❷ *What is the effect on the natural world?*
> ❷ *How does he treat his people differently to the nations?*
> ❷ *What effect does the vision have on Habakkuk (v 8, 16a)?*
> ❷ *How does this vision challenge your view of what God is like?*

---- **TIME OUT** --------------------------------

Read Revelation 6:12-16

> ❷ *How does this echo what Habakkuk saw?*

⌄ Apply

When God comes in final judgement on this world, it will be utterly terrifying. If we trust in Christ, although we will be saved from this judgment, we should still "worship God acceptably with reverence and awe" (Hebrews 12:28).

Pray for such a right attitude to God; and for love to warn others of what is coming.

Rejoice in the Lord

With Amazon Prime it's next-day delivery. With Netflix it's all 10 seasons up to watch whenever you want. We don't do waiting any more. But faith does. It has to.

Wait with patience

Read Habakkuk 3:16b-19

In judgment the Babylonians would invade the land of Judah. But Habakkuk knew that one day God's judgment would fall on the invaders too.

> ❓ *What did he resolve to do (v 16b)?*
> ❓ *How is his attitude different now to what it was in chapter 1?*

✔ Apply

As we look at evil and suffering in the world, and in our own lives, it's not wrong to question God, as Habakkuk did at first. But the answers God gives should help us move on to the patient waiting of chapter 3.

Expect hard times

Dark days lay ahead for the people of Judah.

> ❓ *How would the Babylonian invasion affect the economy (v 17)?*

These hardships were going to hit all God's people in Judah, including Habakkuk and the rest of the "righteous through faith" remnant.

✔ Apply

We live in a world under God's judgment. A world ravaged by sickness and death, disease and disability, war and conflict, tragedy and sorrow, work pressures and relationship breakdown. As believers we do not escape these hardships.

Rejoice in the Lord

> ❓ *What was Habakkuk's resolve in the midst of these trials (v 18-19)?*

Verse 19 is a picture of victory (see Psalm 18:33). Even in the hardest of circumstances, we can experience victory as we rejoice in the Lord and find our strength in him.

✔ Apply

> ❓ *What difficulties are you, or is a believer you know, facing at the moment?*
> ❓ *What does it mean to rejoice in the Lord and find strength in him?*

The musical instruction at the end of Habakkuk 3:19 (and also v 1) indicates that chapter 3 was actually a song to sustain God's people through the dark days that lay ahead. The book begins with complaint and ends in joy; begins with frustration and ends in faith; begins with perplexity and ends in praise, despite many troubles.

⌃ Pray

For now we sing songs in the night. But we do so knowing that soon the eternal dawn will come, day will break, and the sun will rise, when our Saviour comes. Pray for this perspective.

EPHESIANS: Greatest story

It's been said that there is nothing more sublime in the whole of Scripture than Ephesians. That's a big claim—so, buckle up and enjoy the ride!

Seeing Life in Ephesus

Now part of modern-day Turkey, Ephesus was then a Roman provincial capital—and in Acts 18 – 20 we read of the apostle Paul's time in the city (around 53-55 AD). After an initial visit, he later returned to encourage the new Christians there.

Read Acts 19:1, 23-36

- ❓ *What was Ephesus known for?*
- ❓ *What were the different reactions when people became Christians (also v 17-20)?*
- ❓ *Imagine being part of the first church that emerged in the city. What did you see all around you? What might being a Christian in Ephesus have felt like?*

Seeing life in Christ

The letter we call Ephesians was probably written around 60-62 AD, five to seven years after the visit above.

Read Ephesians 1:1-2

- ❓ *What do you notice about Paul's emphasis as he describes himself?*

As we go on, we'll see that the will of God is going to be very important in this letter.

- ❓ *What is Paul's emphasis as he describes and greets his readers?*

As the footnote for verse 1 says, some of the earliest copies of this letter didn't have any reference to Ephesus. Coupled with the lack of mentions of specific people/problems, it's likely that this became Paul's discipleship manual for growing healthy churches across the wider region.

Read Ephesians 1:3

- ❓ *What is Paul focusing his readers' gaze on as he begins?*
- ❓ *Is this a present or future reality?*

The "heavenly realms" was another phrase for spiritual reality. Paul is pulling back the curtain and showing us that there is more to life than meets the eye.

▾ Apply

- ❓ *Where are you in life as you begin this journey through Ephesians? What do you "see" all around you? How do you feel about life as a Christian in light of this?*

Life in Ephesus—as in most of the cities of Asia Minor—would have felt challenging for Christians. Paul doesn't play down those challenges, but points through them to show us the spiritual reality: life in Christ as part of God's eternal story.

▲ Pray

Spend some time praying to the "God and Father of our Lord Jesus Christ" (v 3), asking that as we journey through Ephesians he would lift your gaze, and warm your heart. Pray you would learn to see beyond the life around us, to God's story and the spiritual realities of life in Christ Jesus.

Here on purpose

After his opening greeting, Paul takes a deep breath and begins a sentence that stretches all the way to 1:14. We're just going to look at the first half of it today…

Before the dawn of time

We saw yesterday that Paul begins by pulling open the curtains and showing us spiritual reality. In the "heavenly realms" we've been given "every spiritual blessing in Christ" (v 3). Now we're going to be given a taste of those blessings.

Read Ephesians 1:3-8

- ❓ *What's the tone of this opening section? If you had to choose a soundtrack for these verses, what would it be?*
- ❓ *Make a list of all the different "spiritual blessings" Paul mentions in our passage.*
- ❓ *Which ones do you understand?*
- ❓ *Which ones are you not sure about?*
- ❓ *Sometimes the language of being "predestined" (v 5) or of God "choosing" (v 4) is treated as being negative or exclusive. How do you think Paul wanted the Ephesians to feel as they read verses 4-5?*
- ❓ *"God won't stop loving you, because there was never a beginning to his love for you". How does this statement take you deeper into why Paul writes like he does here?*

How's your praise life?

- ❓ *Make a list of all the words that articulate God's character or posture towards us. What strikes you?*
- ❓ *Count how many times "Christ" (or an equivalent, i.e. "in him", "in whom") is mentioned in these verses.*

- ❓ *How does this give weight to the way Paul ends verse 3?*
- ❓ *Ultimately, why should God be praised?*

This is a spectacular way to begin a letter. Rather than going straight in with tackling ground-level problems, Paul first lifts our horizons to all that we have in Christ. Even before the world was set in motion, God had a staggering plan to bless us through Jesus!

- ❓ *What difference might this make to a Christian reading this who is feeling weak and insignificant?*

✉ Apply

- ❓ *What impact does Paul's praise have on you as you prepare to begin Ephesians?*
- ❓ *If we spent more time looking at our life in the "heavenly realms", how might it change how we feel about life?*
- ❓ *What can prevent us from believing these blessings are "really real"?*

⌃ Pray

Spend some time joining in with Paul's praise as he begins the letter. Choose a couple of the particular blessings Paul lists, and rejoice in them being true for all who are in Christ.

It's all about Jesus

If someone asked you what God was doing in the world, how would you answer? How might your non-believing friends answer that question?

Ephesians begins by bowling us over with the spiritual blessings God has showered upon us in Christ. But as we read on through Paul's incredibly rich opening sentence (1:3-14), we begin to see that, while we've been incredibly blessed, it's certainly not us who's at the heart of God's purposes...

Plan A

Read Ephesians 1:8b-10

❷ *How do these verses connect with yesterday's passage?*

In the first century, the word "mystery" didn't mean something strange and spooky but something that was unknown in the past, but has now been revealed.

❷ *What is the "mystery" that has been made known?*
❷ *Who knows it and who made it known?*
❷ *What has God been planning all along?*
❷ *What is the timescale here? What has happened in verses 9-10?*
❷ *What hasn't yet happened?*

The language of bringing "unity to all things … under Christ" (v 10) has the sense of everything being summed up under a single authority—Jesus Christ.

Both the heavenly realms (1:3, 20; 2:6; 3:10; 6:12) and the realm of earth (1:10; 3:15; 4:9; 6:3) are mentioned a lot in Ephesians. We've already seen that "in Christ" believers now enjoy "every spiritual blessing" in the heavenly realms (1:3). It's as if Paul picks these two categories as they represent the totality of the created world. And it presupposes that Christ's role is not simply to help reconcile earth and heaven, as people "get right with God". Rather he is right at the centre of God's purposes for everything. Indeed, in each realm Christ's authority needs to be seen: there are wayward spiritual powers (2:2-3; 6:10-20) that need to be brought under Christ (1:19-22), and humanity itself needs to be reunited through Christ (2:11-22).

❷ *Given the different pressures of life in Ephesus that we saw two days ago, how do you think Paul's first readers would have felt as they read this?*

⌄ Apply

❷ *How do you feel about the idea of God having a plan?*
❷ *Maybe we tend to think about God having a plan for our own lives, or for our church's. How should it change your perspective to see that God has a plan for the whole cosmos?*
❷ *Can you imagine a universe where everything is centred on and reunited around Christ? What would that be like?*
❷ *Do you ever talk about Jesus as if he were God's "Plan B"?*

Heed and ponder

Pondering what this psalm sets before us will be a tremendous help to us in the ups and downs of our lives.

Four stories, one story

The body of this psalm consists of four very similar stories of trouble and rescue, after which there is a rather different section (v 33-42) and a closing verse. Keep this structure in mind as you...

Read Psalm 107

The four stories each begin with distress that provokes prayer, which is answered and issues in joy and thanksgiving. These are not four separate stories: they are told by the same redeemed and gathered people. They tell the one story of God's rescue in four vivid and complementary ways. As we read them, remember that we too are "exiles, scattered" (1 Peter 1:1), and that the Lord Jesus is the one who has wonderfully redeemed and gathered us.

> ❷ *For each of these four stories ask yourself: a) why God's people were in distress, and b) how the Lord rescued them.*
> 1. *Lost in a wasteland world (Psalm 107:4-9)*
> 2. *Trapped in a dark world (v 10-16)*
> 3. *Weak in a sick world (v 17-22)*
> 4. *Scared in a dangerous world (v 23-32)*

The final surprise

Read Psalm 107:33-43 again

> ❷ *What is the pattern here of good times and bad times?*

> ❷ *Who is in charge of both?*

The surprise at this point in the psalm is that we do not have a fifth scene following the same pattern. Instead, we find God taking his people through both hard times and good times. Notice that it is God who does both. The bad times do not just happen: God allows them. This is why the wise need to "ponder" these things: for every one of the events described, both hard and good, are "the loving deeds of the LORD" (v 43).

⏷ Apply

As I write this, a third of the world is in some kind of lockdown due to the COVID-19 coronavirus.

> ❷ *What perspective does Psalm 107 give us on the COVID-19 pandemic?*
> ❷ *Do you find it hard to trust that all things, both hard and good, are "the loving deeds of the LORD"?*

God has promised that he will make each one of his people like the Lord Jesus in character (Romans 8:29). This is the "good" that he is always working for in those who love him (Romans 8:28). We sometimes wish that it did not have to hurt so much. But our Christlikeness, not our comfort, is God's aim. He has promised to do it, that we may be blessed, in becoming more like Jesus, with whom we will be in the end. And, however much it may hurt in this life, we shall see then that it has been worth it.

From me to you

Remember, despite often being separated in our English Bibles, these verses are still part of the long sentence that Paul began in verse 3…

… but their particular focus means they're often treated separately.

God's big picture
Read Ephesians 1:11-14

> ❓ How does the subject of these verses change from v 11 to v 13 to v 14?
> ❓ Who does Paul have in mind each time?
> ❓ How does this change in subject clarify for us Paul's overall point here?
> ❓ Does the language of God's work in verse 11 remind you of anything we've seen so far?
> ❓ What is the end result of God's work amongst Jewish believers (v 12)?

The language of being "chosen" takes us back to the Old Testament's emphasis that Israel was God's "portion" (e.g. Psalm 33:12 or Deuteronomy 4:20). The family line of Abraham had been given God's great promises—and as such many put their "hope in Christ", longing in faith for God's rescuing "Messiah". This was all part of God's plan for his glory (Ephesians 1:11-12).

God's big deposit

> ❓ According to verse 13, how did the recipients of this letter get included in God's plan?
> ❓ When did they receive the Holy Spirit?
> ❓ How does Paul see the Spirit's role, and what are we still waiting for (v 13-14)?

The Holy Spirit is a "deposit" of our future salvation—and what a particularly fitting deposit! Staggeringly, Paul speaks not just of Christians inheriting God, but God possessing us (v 14). The Spirit's presence gives us a foretaste of this relationship as we wait (1:15-23 will give us more on this!).

> ❓ How does the repetition in verses 12 and 14 show God's ultimate purpose here?

Given the transition from Israel ("we"), to Gentiles ("you"), to both ("our"), it's wonderful that Paul places that repeated refrain where he does. For him, there's no ultimate distinction and it's all part of the same gracious plan.

✔ Apply

> ❓ How has this opening section from verses 2-14 helped you see what you have in Christ?
> ❓ How might a proud Jewish-background Christian have been tempted to respond to Paul's teaching here? What would a healthy response have been?
> ❓ How should a Gentile-background Christian (like many of us) respond to Paul's teaching here?

Eyes wide open

What do we really need to flourish as Christians today? If you were putting together a "wish list" of essential spiritual tools for 21st-century disciples, what would be on it?

We have spectacular spiritual blessings in Christ—all part of God's eternal plan to bring everything under Jesus. Paul now turns to pray for his readers. We'll see that at the heart of his prayer are two requests, which are really bound up with each other.

Request #1

Read Ephesians 1:15-17

Like in most of his letters, Paul encourages his readers by giving thanks for the signs of God's work in their lives (v 15-16). But it's in what Paul then prays for these Christians that we get a real insight into what he thinks is crucial for them to spiritually survive and thrive.

- ❓ *What does Paul ask for (v 17)?*
- ❓ *What is the ultimate purpose of his request (v 17)?*
- ❓ *How does this prayer request show how reliant we are on God?*

☑ Apply

- ❓ *Does Paul's request surprise you? Why do you think it is so crucial?*
- ❓ *When was the last time you prayed like this for yourself or someone else?*

Request #2

Read Ephesians 1:18-19a

Paul's second request is also about "knowing".

- ❓ *What are the three things that Paul wants the Ephesians to "know"?*
- ❓ *What do you think each of these means?*
- ❓ *How do these three things connect to Ephesians 1:3-14?*
- ❓ *What strikes you about the nature of this "knowing"? Where does it take place and what does God need to do?*

Paul wants us to know God's eternal plan—all that has already been done in Christ—deep within our being, so that it changes us from the inside out. Ephesians is going to be a spectacular tour through God's plan—but it's not for the faint-hearted! This "knowledge" means nothing can be the same again.

☑ Apply

- ❓ *What would a church look like that was hungry to know God and his eternal plan better?*
- ❓ *Do you value "knowing" with the "eyes of your hearts" (v 18), rather than just cognitive understanding?*
- ❓ *What would a church look like that was hungry to know God with the "eyes of their heart"?*

☑ Pray

Take some time to pray through this prayer for yourself. Slowly pause on each phrase and ask God for his mercy in answering your prayer. Pray it through for those you love.

Jesus above all

Paul has just prayed for God to give us a "heart knowledge" of his glorious eternal plan. Now Paul starts to show how this letter is his own answer to that prayer.

Read Ephesians 1:19b-21

- ❓ *Where has God's power taken Jesus Christ from and to?*
- ❓ *How high would this score on a "Cosmic Power" scale?*
- ❓ *What position in our universe does Jesus Christ now have (v 20-21)?*

Christ being seated at God's right hand picks up on God's promise to David in Psalm 110:1. And it's a position not just over human earthly rulers, for "all rule and authority, power and dominion" (Ephesians 1:21) means over spiritual forces in the "heavenly realms" too (see also 6:12; 2:2). Jesus is now above them all.

- ❓ *When does Christ's term of office begin and how long will it last (1:21)?*

☑ Apply

- ❓ *How might that change how you feel about being a Christian today?*

For the church
Read Ephesians 1:22-23

···· TIME OUT ····

Paul quotes Psalm in verse 22. Let's take a look!

Read Psalm 8:3-9

- ❓ *What is our God-given task (v 6)?*

As those uniquely created in the image of God, humanity's purpose was to make visible God's loving rule over his creation.

Read Genesis 1:27-28

- ❓ *What does humanity's original "imaging" task involve in verse 28?*
- ❓ *Do you notice any similarities with the language of Ephesians 1:22-23?*

Sadly, humanity has failed to be faithful image-bearers that fill the earth with a knowledge of God. Yet Paul's allusion to Psalm 8:6 in Ephesians 1:22 shows us that Jesus Christ is the new head of humanity for this same purpose.

- ❓ *Originally humanity was to "fill the earth" by procreation—making more image-bearing babies! But according to verse 23, how does Jesus "fill the earth"?*
- ❓ *What is the breathtaking scope of this "filling" (v 23)?*

☑ Apply

We're going to see that God's cosmic work through the church, a new humanity, is crucial to Ephesians (see 3:10)—which helps open our eyes to the importance of the church in God's plan.

But even more crucial is the fact that Jesus is our universe-filling head—raised above all!

- ❓ *God's plan hasn't been left on the drawing board! How will this encourage you today?*

This is your life

Are you ever tempted to assume that the success of God's purposes relies on the ability or resourcefulness of the people involved, i.e. Christians?

If so, Ephesians 2:1-3 is going to mean we're in for a shock! Chapter 2 will give us two different camera angles on the difference that God's work has already made for those who are "in Christ".

Welcome to the morgue

This may be a very familiar passage to you. As we walk through it slowly, try and let the reality of the words impact upon you. Imagine you're reading it for the first time!

Read Ephesians 2:1-2

The word for "transgressions" (v 1; "tres-passes", ESV) captures individual acts of breaking God's law or violating his will, whereas "sins" suggests a general description of rebelling against God.

- ❓ *What images come to mind as you read the description here?*
- ❓ *What was the Ephesians' spiritual state?*
- ❓ *Are we passive or active in these verses?*

"The ruler of the kingdom of the air" (v 2) uses the language of a local leader to describe the devil and his spiritual influence. "Air" was the sphere between earth and heaven, suggesting spiritual power that impinges on earth.

Looking in the mirror

As in 1:11-14, Paul initially distinguishes between the Ephesians as Gentiles and himself as a Jewish believer (2:1: "As for you...").

Read Ephesians 2:3

- ❓ *Who is Paul now including?*
- ❓ *How much wriggle-room is there for people to exclude themselves from this diagnosis?*

"Flesh" does not mean our physical bodies but the human inclination to rebel against God. Therefore this isn't just about our sexual desires but all self-focused thoughts and wants.

- ❓ *Are we passive or active in verse 3?*
- ❓ *How does verse 3 clarify whether humanity is culpable for their situation?*

"Wrath" is not an irrational passion or quick-tempered anger, nor just "one side" of God's character. Rather, in the face of our rebellion and self-driven evil, God's unswerving and perfect character displays itself in a pure, loving and deserved judgment against sinners, expressed ultimately at judgment day.

- ❓ *How do you feel about this diagnosis?*

Apply

- ❓ *Do you find it easy to agree that this is a fair description of you without Christ?*
- ❓ *Where in our culture do we see evidence that v 1-3 is true? Where in our culture is it effectively asserted that v 1-3 is false?*
- ❓ *The concept of "freedom" is highly prized in Western culture. According to these verses, in what ways are we not free?*

Raised with Christ

We've seen the stark reality of our predicament. If God is going to accomplish his plan, then something remarkable needs to happen.

Loved to life

Like yesterday, we may "know" these verses well—but do we know them with the "eyes of our hearts"?

Read Ephesians 2:4-7

- ❷ *What prompts God's action, according to verse 4? How is this point emphasised?*
- ❷ *Do verses 5-7 remind you of anything so far in Ephesians? (Hint: see 1:19-21.)*
- ❷ *Where are Christians now? Does this surprise you? How does it connect back to 1:3?*
- ❷ *According to 2:7, what is the future for Christian believers?*
- ❷ *How does our new situation contrast with our previous state in 2:1-3?*

"Grace" (v 5, 7, 8) is a word that Christians use a lot—and Paul clearly sees it as being a central feature of the gospel. It speaks of an incredible gift, but one that isn't deserved.

Credit where credit's due

Read Ephesians 2:8-10

- ❷ *What do these verses add?*
- ❷ *What attitude or behaviour is ruled out (v 8-9)?*
- ❷ *How does the language of verse 10 help you marvel at the scope of what God has done for us?*

⌄ Apply

Remember Paul's prayer for us to know God and his plan better—including our hope, our inheritance and God's power for us (1:15-19)?

- ❷ *How has reading 2:1-10 begun to answer that prayer for you?*
- ❷ *How do you tend to imagine God sees you? As a struggling sinner? A lost cause? Not really worth his effort?*
- ❷ *How can this passage help you to be convinced that "God is for you"?*

⌃ Pray

Spend some time dwelling upon God's character as shown in verse 4. Join in the praise to our God for his glorious grace.

United with Christ

Our world can seem more fragmented now than ever before. People are therefore desperate to bring about unity.

But that often feels impossible! Humanity is full of so many tensions, rivalries and division. So if God's plan is to bring everything under Christ, including forming a new humanity, "the church" (1:10, 22-23), how is God going to deal with this disunity?

Alienated

Having given us one camera angle on what God has done for us in Christ (2:1-10), now we get the second...

Read Ephesians 2:11-12

- ❓ *Who is Paul especially addressing here (see v 11)?*
- ❓ *What does the "nickname" given to the Gentiles underline about the first-century situation?*
- ❓ *What was this division founded upon, according to verse 12?*
- ❓ *How does this add to the earlier description of the human predicament in verses 1-2?*

Male circumcision was a sign given by God (see Genesis 17) to mark Israel out as separate, God's treasured possession who were to live differently. But now, in first-century Jewish eyes, anyone else was "the uncircumcised". But Paul begins to highlight this was merely an external action ("done in the body") and had served its purpose ("by human hands"). As the Old Testament foretold, God is now doing something different (see Deuteronomy 10:16; 30:6; Jeremiah 4:4).

Reconciled

Read Ephesians 2:13-18

- ❓ *Do you notice any repeated words or ideas in verses 13-17?*
- ❓ *According to verse 13, what has changed? How did it happen?*
- ❓ *Make a list of the different actions in verses 14-16. Who does them?*
- ❓ *What exactly has Jesus' death achieved?*
- ❓ *How is this reconciliation a crucial step in God's overall plan (see 1:9-10)?*

"Peace" means divided things being brought together in harmony, both horizontally, between human groups, and vertically, with God. This is what the OT promised (e.g. see Ezekiel 37:18-19) and what is now proclaimed in the gospel (Ephesians 2:17).

⌄ Apply

- ❓ *Why is the repeated command in v 11-12 important for us. What will it lead to?*

Do you think of Jesus as "our peace" (v 14)? Spend some time meditating upon him as our peace. As you look at your local community, your nation or even the whole world—what tends to stand in the way of human unity?

⌃ Pray

Read verse 18 again and then make the most of it!

A difficult psalm

We struggle when a psalmist prays for his enemies to be punished, and we wonder how we can ever join in this prayer. Psalm 109 is an acute example of this problem.

Read Psalm 109

❓ *What is David's problem (v 1-5)?*

The issue is what is *said* about David. God is "silent", and David longs for him to speak (v 1) for plenty of others have "opened their mouths" against him (v 2). They are "wicked" in their character, motivated by "hatred", and "they accuse" David falsely (v 4) despite the fact that he has shown them "friendship" and done to them nothing but "good" (v 2-5).

Read Psalm 109:6-20 again, keeping in mind that this is a *prayer*, not a *curse*...

❓ *What does he pray against his betrayer?*
❓ *How would this punishment fit the crime, and who would it come from?*

David does not seek to unleash a curse on his enemies; rather, he prays to God about them. He leaves the outcome in God's hands.

☑ Apply

❓ *When people treat you badly, do you retaliate or do you ask for God's help?*
❓ *When might you pray for God to judge?*

Family matters

In verses 9-15 David prays against this man's family. This is the part we find most difficult. David prays that this man's whole family will be "blotted out" and be no more. Why? Because the default convictions and behaviour of the man's family will line up

with the behaviour of the man himself. The spirit of treachery that motivates this man is like a terrible virus infecting his family and all who are influenced by him. Just as a life-threatening virus must be blotted out if the rest of us are to be safe, so all who share this man's heart must be removed.

Even as we consider this general truth, we must remember how the Bible repeatedly gives us glimpses of glorious exceptions. The Moabites were ancient enemies of the people of God, and yet Ruth was converted and came under the wings of the Lord for refuge (Ruth 2:12). There were also physical descendants of the Pharaohs who came into the people of God (Exodus 12:38; 1 Chronicles 4:17-18). This is wonderful. But they had to break their corporate solidarity first, to save themselves from the corrupt family or culture by which they'd been shaped.

The end of treachery

❓ *How and why does David praise God at the conclusion (Psalm 109:30-31)?*
❓ *Will you pray that all treachery against Jesus will be brought to an end?*

David is praying, initially, about his own accusers. But this psalm can also rightly be prayed about all those who accuse God's ultimate King, the Lord Jesus. And this is a prayer that is always answered, whether in the judgment on the persecutor or in the wounds of the Saviour who pays for them.

Home sweet home

After 2000 years of "Gentiles" being part of the Church, it can be easy to rush over these verses and miss the world-shattering news they contain.

Having first established our hopelessness *without Christ* (2:11-12), and having then shown us the powerful reconciling work *of Christ* (2:13-18), Paul now focuses in on the consequences of Jesus' death for God's eternal plan.

Belonging

Read Ephesians 2:19-20

- ❷ *How does verse 19 link to verses 11-18?*
- ❷ *Which imagery and language in verse 19 has already been used in verses 11-18? Which is new?*
- ❷ *Just how different is the situation for Gentile Christians in verse 19, compared to our past in verses 11-12?*
- ❷ *Why do you think Paul includes v 20?*

Being part of a first-century household meant receiving the security and protection of the master. Whereas before, the Gentiles were "without hope" (v 12), now they come under God's own roof!

Building

Read Ephesians 2:21-22

- ❷ *What is "the whole building" (v 21)?*
- ❷ *How does the "household" and building imagery develop in verse 21?*
- ❷ *What is the timescale of this new temple-building project?*
- ❷ *How significant is Jesus in this description? Why?*

To hear Gentiles being called "fellow citizens" would have been shocking, but there was a clear Old Testament expectation that God's grace would reach beyond Israel. Abraham's line would lead to blessing for the nations (e.g. Genesis 12:3) and foreigners would come to God's temple to worship him (see Isaiah 2:1-5; 66:18-20). Of course, what no one expected was that the Gentiles would be part of the temple itself!

🔽 Apply

- ❷ *Given the cultural and historical differences between Gentiles and Jews, what would you have felt were the chances that this new people/household/ temple would stay united?*
- ❷ *How does knowing what God has done help us to stay united?*

Are you ever tempted to feel "not at home" in church or with other Christians? Perhaps you sometimes feel particularly conscious of your past, your upbringing or your circumstances? How should this passage help you?

🔼 Pray

Read Ephesians 2:22 again. Give thanks for this mind-blowing shared privilege—and pray that your church family might have a clear awareness of this over the next few days.

Reveal the mystery

We've seen that God's eternal plan to bring everything together under Christ has been taking shape. But there's one vital step that still needs to happen…

Revealed mystery

Read Ephesians 3:1-6

As we've said, Paul uses the word "mystery" (v 3, 4, 6) not to describe something strange or spooky but something previously unknown but now revealed.

> ❓ *What is Paul's present situation (v 1)?*
> ❓ *How does Paul understand his ministry? What is he doing and who is it for?*
> ❓ *How does verse 5 help us to see the significance of this on the timeline of history?*

In verse 1 Paul breaks off his sentence and it's as if he casts his eyes down to his chains and suddenly recognises the importance of explaining to his readers how this situation isn't a disaster! For the Gentiles, nothing could be more significant than the ministry he has been doing.

Cosmic ministry

Read Ephesians 3:7-13

> ❓ *How does Paul consider his own part in God's plan (v 7-8)?*
> ❓ *What are the two aims and two audiences of Paul's ministry (v 8-9)?*
> ❓ *How have we seen the "boundless riches of Christ" (v 8) in Ephesians so far?*
> ❓ *How do verses 9-11 connect Paul's ministry to God's eternal plan?*

Imagine someone turning to Paul and offering him commiserations for being in a Roman jail cell (v 13). What do you think he might say?

▾ Apply

3:10 is arguably one of the most stunning individual verses in Ephesians. As one writer says, the church is revealed to be "God's pilot scheme for the reconciled universe of the future". As Paul travelled all over the Mediterranean, across land and sea, the breathtaking reality was that his mystery-revealing, body-building ministry was having an impact way beyond even this world.

> ❓ *What difference would it make to your life if you saw church in the same light as Paul in verse 10?*

Gospel ministry often looks weak and is sidelined in the eyes of our culture. To many, as they looked at Paul under imprisonment in Rome around 62 AD, they may have seen a lost cause, a hopeless case of one man taking things a bit too seriously. And yet as he preached Christ and planted churches, a glorious reality was being revealed.

> ❓ *We're not the apostle Paul, but how does this passage encourage us in our own gospel endeavours as individuals and churches?*

Knowing the unknowable

It's fairly standard for Paul to begin his letters with a prayer. But it's much less common for him to stop half way through and pray again! Why would he do that?

Making Christ at home
Read Ephesians 3:14-17a

Paul picks up where he left off in 3:1. The reference to "every family" (v 15) is a wordplay on "Father" (v 14). Paul prays because everyone and everything is under God's authority—whether in the heavenly realms or on earth.

> ❷ *What is Paul's initial request (v 16)?*
> ❷ *What is its goal (v 17a)?*

The language of dwelling speaks of Christ "making his home" in our lives—an on-going residency with accompanying renovations! Thankfully God's Spirit (v 16) is "on the job", establishing Christ increasingly at the "heart" of all we are and do.

Blown away by love
Read Ephesians 3:17b-19

> ❷ *Can you try putting Paul's second request in your own words (v 17b-19a)?*
> ❷ *How have chapters 1 – 3 helped us to be "rooted and established in love" (v 17)?*

When did you last stop and revel in God's love for you? Paul imagines it in four-dimensional terms! Christ's love is so *wide* that he graciously accepts any sinner; so *long* that it is an eternal commitment; so *high* that it seats us alongside him in the heavenly realms; so *deep* that he stooped to a barbaric cross to pay for our sins.

> ❷ *What is the ultimate goal of Paul's second prayer (v 19b)?*

Humanity is divided and alienated from God, hell-bent on its own desires (2:1-3). But as we come under Christ and bask in his glorious plan, we are transformed by this "4D" love. Here Paul again uses the evocative imagery of "filling" (see also 1:23). It takes us back to humanity's task of "filling" the earth with the blessing of God's rule, as well as to the Jerusalem temple being "filled" with God's glory (e.g. Ezekiel 43:1-12). Remarkably, as God's new humanity are transformed by Christ's love, we experience that same filling.

Power source
Read Ephesians 3:20-21

> ❷ *Why is the church mentioned in verse 21?*
> ❷ *How can these verses help us when we're not feeling motivated to pray?*

⌃ Pray

This prayer helps us to see more clearly what God wants to do in us. You are Christ's "home address" (v 17)!

Take some time to slowly echo Paul's prayer for yourself and Christians you know, letting it challenge your own priorities and goals. You may find it helpful to write or draw it out.

The masterplan

Ephesians is a book of two halves. In the first half Paul has laid out God's breathtaking plan to bring everything together under Christ. Now we see how it shapes everything…

At the heart of God's eternal plan is a new humanity, Christ's body, the "fullness of him who fills everything in every way" (1:23). But what difference should this truth make to us?

One plan

Read Ephesians 4:1

- ❓ *How would you put verse 1 into your own words?*
- ❓ *How is Paul gearing us up to respond to chapters 1 – 3?*
- ❓ *Why would Paul reference being "a prisoner for the Lord" again (see 3:1)?*

"Live a life" (4:1) is often translated "walk" (ESV). It comes up four more times in this half of Ephesians (4:17; 5:2, 8, 15). Though we once "walked" in sin and death (2:1-2), God has saved us to "walk" in the good works he has prepared (2:10).

One love

Ephesians has unveiled a cosmic plan that impacts upon both the spiritual and the earthly realms—and we've been "called" into it (1:18). There's nothing like it! So how do we live lives "worthy" of this calling?

Read Ephesians 4:2-3

- ❓ *What attitude should we have (v 2)?*
- ❓ *Why is this necessary?*
- ❓ *Why are we called to "keep the unity…" (v 3), rather than "be united" or "achieve unity"?*

- ❓ *How does this difference effect how we put it into practice?*
- ❓ *How does Paul root this appeal in the language and truths of chapters 1 – 3?*

One body

Read Ephesians 4:4-6

- ❓ *What point is Paul trying to persuade us of?*
- ❓ *What might disunity among Christians reveal about God and our knowledge of his plan?*

✓ Apply

Through chapters 4 – 6, we'll see Paul apply the reality of God's plan into every corner and sphere of our lives. But first, he chooses to focus on something very ordinary: love and staying united. Perhaps we might be tempted to do a "double take". Isn't there something more dramatic or "spiritual"?

- ❓ *How do you feel as you read the simplicity of Paul's challenge? Do you take this as seriously as Paul does?*

▲ Pray

Spend some time reflecting on the character descriptions in 4:2. Examine your own heart.

How are these a "worthy" (v 1) response to all that God has done in chapters 1 – 3?

Dealing with division

Imagine you were moving to a new place. What would you look for in a church? Now think about this: why would you look for those things? Why are they so important?

Gifts from the King

Read Ephesians 4:7-10

Having established our "oneness" as Christ's body (v 4), Paul now addresses "each one of us" (v 7), appealing to us as individuals.

> ❷ *What is the general principle that Paul is establishing in verse 7?*

Psalm 68 speaks of the triumph of God's rescuing king. According to verse 8, who is the fulfilment of this character and what has he done?

> ❷ *How does Paul prove this "ascended" King is Jesus Christ in verses 9-10?*

As in 1:23, Jesus' ascension above every rule and authority is bound up in God's eternal plan of him "filling"—here explicitly "the whole universe" (4:10)!

Words for the body

Read Ephesians 4:11-13

> ❷ *What is the nature of the gifts Jesus has given to his people (v 11)?*
> ❷ *What do they have in common?*

The original phrasing of "the pastors and teachers" means they're closely linked and may even be a combined role. Christians have different views on whether God provides people in all four roles in every generation. Given Paul's earlier descrip-tion of "the foundation of the apostles and prophets" (2:20), some conclude these refer here to the writers of the Old Testament ("prophets") and those authorised to write the New Testament ("apostles"). Others see prophets as less authoritative "gospel encouragers" (e.g. 1 Corinthians 14:3).

> ❷ *Try sketching out Ephesians 4:11-13 as a chain of action. What happens in each step?*
> ❷ *Are you surprised by any of them?*

"Service" (v 12) is sometimes translated "ministry".

> ❷ *According to Paul, who "does ministry"?*
> ❷ *How does this change our mindset about church?*
> ❷ *How would you put verse 13 into your own words?*

Apply

> ❷ *Where are you on the chain in verses 11-13? How could you play your part with your church family today?*
> ❷ *What difference might it make to your relationship with your church leaders to see that God gives us people (v 11), rather than skills or abilities?*
> ❷ *How does this passage effect your perspective on the "why" of a church gathering/service?*

Maturity that matters

Every church would say that they strive for spiritual maturity—but what is God's plan for growing healthy churches?

Danger: Infants at sea!

Paul has just described Christ's plan for his church: to become a "mature" body that attains to the "whole measure of the fullness of Christ" (v 13). But now he warns us about what will happen if we don't take this plan seriously.

Read Ephesians 4:14

- ❓ *What emotions and reactions do you think Paul's imagery is meant to evoke?*
- ❓ *What is the particular danger facing us?*
- ❓ *Why does Paul describe the intent behind the threat, as well as the threat itself?*

Does the language remind you of any other danger that God's people face in the Bible? (If not, take a look at Genesis 3:1,13; Ephesians 6:11; 2 Corinthians 11:3)

The truth in love

Read Ephesians 4:15-16

- ❓ *What is God's solution to the threat of verse 14? Where does this go on the chain we sketched from verses 11-13?*
- ❓ *How does truth and love (v 15) contrast with verse 14?*
- ❓ *Given the chain of verses 11-13, who do you think Paul means by "supporting ligaments" and "each part" in verse 16?*
- ❓ *How does verse 16 take us back to verse 7?*

☑ Apply

If we've been badly hurt by a church, then we may be hesitant about committing to one again. Love should be pulsating through the veins of everything a church does—and we need to repent where that hasn't been the case.

Yet Paul says it is absolutely necessary for every church's flourishing—and every Christian's flourishing—that there is a commitment to speaking the truth in love (v 15). This isn't about simply "telling the truth", but speaking King Jesus' words (v 11), found in Scripture and which are "full" of Christ (v 13). Suddenly the need for humility, gentleness, patience and bearing with one another makes sense (v 2)! If we're bruised, it may also take time. But we still each have a vital part to play in fulfilling God's purposes for his new humanity, through local churches.

- ❓ *Would you be strong enough to resist teaching that undermines or dilutes the biblical gospel? How might our answer to this question reveal our own need to hear afresh Paul's warning in verse 14?*
- ❓ *How can churches or individuals be more effective at "truthing in love"?*
- ❓ *Where do you need to grow in this area?*
- ❓ *According to verses 15-16, what are the different dynamics to a church's relationship to Jesus? Do you think about your church's relationship with Jesus like this?*

King and priest

Psalm 110 is quoted or alluded to an extraordinary number of times in the New Testament, like a web page choc-a-bloc with hyperlinks to other parts of the web.

Read Psalm 110

- ❓ *Who is speaking in verses 1, 3 and 4?*
- ❓ *What do we learn about the king's enemies?*
- ❓ *Who will have the final victory?*

In the Old Testament, David's enemies were nations such as Philistia, Moab, Edom, Assyria and Babylon. But these were just representatives of a universally rebellious human race. All of us, by nature, refuse to have God's King rule over us. We're determined to make our own decisions about our jobs, sexual relationships, possessions, money, or rights. The idea that our freedom could be constrained by some external power telling us what to do sounds abhorrent.

☑ Apply

- ❓ *Think of anyone you know who hates the idea of God telling them what to do. How can you show them that God's rule is a good thing?*
- ❓ *When do you struggle with God's rule over your own life?*

The king who is a priest

In verse 4 God promises that the king will be "a priest … in the order of Melchizedek". In Genesis 14, Melchizedek was the priest-king of Salem (later Jerusalem). He blessed Abraham, who gave him an offering, a tithe. And so the great patriarch acknowledged that this priest-king foreshadowed in his unique person someone who would be greater than Abraham—who would have the greatness to bless Abraham and to whom it was right that Abraham gave a tithe.

TIME OUT

Melchizedek ruled a people (as king) and gave to his people the astonishing privilege of access to God (by his priestly role). Read the explanation of all this in Hebrews 7.

We tend to think that kingship is more important than priesthood. But it is because this king is a priest that everything else follows; for kingship is exercised on behalf of God over people, whereas priesthood is exercised towards God on behalf of people. Only because this king would offer a sacrifice to atone for the sins of his people can he lead a people whose hearts will be transformed deep within.

☐ Pray

We had to wait until Jesus of Nazareth came to see this King-Priest walk the earth, announcing the kingdom of God in his own person, offering himself as the sacrifice as he, our great High Priest, and making atonement for the sins of all who trust in him.

Turn these thoughts into thanksgiving and praise.

Who do you think you are?

We live in an age of personal reinvention. We can sculpt bodies, change wardrobes, and edit profiles. But have we really changed where it really matters?

Who you were

We've seen that the original readers of Ephesians weren't from a Jewish background (see 2:11; 1:11-13). Paul has already painted their former lives very starkly (2:1-2; 2:11-12)— and now he shows them that it's inconceivable for them to go back to that way of life.

Read Ephesians 4:17-19

As in 4:1, "live" in verse 17 means "walk", emphasising how we carry out our day-to-day lives.

> ❓ *List the different ways that Gentiles are described in verses 17-19. Does anything surprise you?*
> ❓ *What is the heart of their problem?*
> ❓ *Why would the diagnosis of verses 18-19 persuade you of verse 17?*

Many of us will be from a "Gentile" background too, and you may struggle with Paul's description here. Maybe we feel that the non-Christians we know are very intelligent, cultured and well-behaved.

> ❓ *Is Paul ruling this out?*
> ❓ *So what is the "darkened mind" he is referring to really about?*
> ❓ *Christians are sometimes accused of having views that "belong in the dark ages". Why is this accusation tragically ironic, given verse 18?*

Who you are

Read Ephesians 4:20-24

> ❓ *What repeated ideas do you notice in this section?*
> ❓ *What do you make of Paul's summary of someone becoming a Christian in verses 20-21, 24?*
> ❓ *Do verses 22-24 seem to be a one-off event, an ongoing process, or both?*

The need for inward renewal (v 23) was underlined by Paul's prayers in 1:18 and 3:16. As one writer puts it, "learning Christ means welcoming him as a living person and being shaped by his teaching".

✓ Apply

Our culture says: "Do what feels good" ... "Be yourself" ... "Just be you".

> ❓ *In light of this passage, how do you think Paul would engage with these common soundbites?*
> ❓ *We can sometimes think of unbelief as simply an intellectual matter—or of unbelievers as "morally neutral". How does Paul's diagnosis challenge this view?*
> ❓ *Who do you think you look more like—your "new humanity" or your "old humanity"?*
> ❓ *What do you need to remember as you "walk" day by day?*

The life of love

Love is a word we can use without thinking about what it involves. It can get associated with extraordinary acts or gifts, rather than everyday attitudes and behaviour.

But, for Paul, love is not something that happens around the edges of our lives. Christians have been "rooted and established in love" (3:17). It is knowing the "four-dimensional" richness of Christ's love that will lead to being "filled to the measure of all the fullness of God" (3:19). So it's no surprise that displaying this love of Christ matters...

We're going to read today's passage as a whole, before breaking it down.

Read Ephesians 4:25 – 5:2

❓ *How does 4:25 connect this passage to the previous section?*

❓ *Make a list of all the different motivations for a Christian's behaviour here. How do they connect to what we've seen in Ephesians 1 – 3?*

❓ *Who are these relationships between (Ephesians 4:25, 29, 32)?*

Body talk
Read Ephesians 4:25-29 again

❓ *Why would lying, anger and stealing be so dangerous for God's people?*

❓ *How does verse 27 remind us that resisting anger is more than an internal battle?*

❓ *How can our day-to-day work be a means of loving others?*

❓ *In what ways should our speech be shaped by love?*

Love exemplified
Read Ephesians 4:30 – 5:2 again

❓ *Given the Holy Spirit's role in 2:22 and 4:3, why does verse 30 fit so well here?*

❓ *How do verses 31-32 flesh this out?*

❓ *What/who is our model as we seek to love our brothers and sisters (4:32 – 5:2)?*

❓ *How is this emphasised?*

✓ Apply

This passage presents us with a stark contrast: we can either work *with* the Holy Spirit in building up Christ's body, or we can effectively support the devil in working *against* God's purposes. Yet we do so from the security of being "dearly loved children" who long to show the "family likeness" (5:1).

❓ *Is this contrast a new idea for you? Would you think about it in these terms on a daily basis?*

❓ *Do you really believe that your words, your work and your willingness to forgive all play a part in God's eternal plan?*

❓ *How will this passage affect your approach to others in your church family this week?*

Distorted love

Have you ever heard the illustration about the frog that gets boiled in water because it doesn't notice the gradual rising temperature in the pan?

It speaks to our unthinking tendency to "acclimatise" to our surroundings.

Out of place
Read Ephesians 5:3-4

❓ *What does Paul forbid in verse 3?*
❓ *What motivation is given?*

"Sexual immorality" (v 3) meant any kind of sexual activity outside of the covenant union of heterosexual marriage. Paul sometimes describes this as "impurity", but here he also imagines a broader category of behaviour (v 3: "any kind", NIV, or "all", ESV).

❓ *It's not unusual for sexual immorality to be justified under the rationale of "love". How does this "love" contrast with the God-like love of verses 1-2?*
❓ *What do the three unacceptable things in verse 4 have in common?*
❓ *What is the "positive" alternative that Paul highlights in v 4b? How might this help us guard against the sins of v 4a?*

Are you serious?
Read Ephesians 5:5-7

❓ *How do these verses connect to verses 3-4?*

The phrasing of verse 5 implies consistent behaviour that effectively defines a person.

❓ *Why would someone who is consistently sexually immoral, impure or greedy be guilty of worshipping idols (v 5)?*

❓ *What makes this so serious?*

Paul is not saying that *anyone* who struggles with these sins is automatically excluded from God's kingdom, but if we've given ourselves over to them without any signs of repentance, then we should be concerned.

❓ *How will seeing ourselves as part of Christ's kingdom change our perspective on our behaviour?*

We're not to share in the immoral activities of our culture, because we're now partners in the promise of the gospel (v 7; 3:6).

⌄ Apply

❓ *Do you have the same "not-even-a-hint" approach as Paul in 5:3-4?*

There will be good reasons to talk sensitively and positively about God's good design for sex. We're not called to be prudish or create a pastorally unhelpful "sex vacuum" in our teaching. But is your tendency to take verse 4 either "too far" or "not far enough"?

❓ *What "empty words" (v 6) does our culture utter about sex? What makes such "words" easy to be deceived by?*

⌃ Pray

Give thanks (v 4) for your situation, whether single, married or exploring marriage. Ask for God's help in the struggles you face. Pray that you would worship our generous God, rather than gratifying yourself.

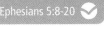

Sleeping with the light on

Turning on the lights can be a confrontational experience—especially when it involves looking in the bathroom mirror first thing in the morning!

Today Paul will use the contrasting imagery of light and darkness to help us think about our own behaviour.

Light fantastic
Read Ephesians 5:8-14

- ❷ How does this contrast show what has and should change?
- ❷ What is being exposed in verse 11?
- ❷ How might this happen?

There is a slight translation variation in v 13-14a. The ESV emphasises things being made *visible*, but the NIV goes further: "everything that is illuminated becomes a light". This transformation has been the Ephesian Christians' own journey (v 8). What follows is probably an early Christian song (v 14b), featuring words from the prophet Isaiah (see Isaiah 26:19 and 60:1), calling unbelievers to come into the light of Christ.

Apply

- ❷ How does the light and darkness imagery impact your pursuit of godliness?
- ❷ Can you recall times when Christians' "fruit of the light" (Ephesians 5:9) has exposed "deeds of darkness" (v 11)? Has this led to the unbeliever waking up (v 14b) and turning to Christ?
- ❷ How does verse 11a challenge you?
- ❷ When does such behaviour occupy your mind and lips (v 12)?

Under the influence
Read Ephesians 5:15-20

- ❷ Given all we've seen, what could "making the most of every opportunity" mean (v 16)?
- ❷ What should a Christians' life be shaped by in verse 17? How have we seen this in Ephesians (e.g. see 1:9-10; 4:1)?
- ❷ Having warned against drunkenness, how should Christians be "under the influence" (5:18)?!

"Be filled with the Spirit" (v 18) is often taken as a command to be "full" of the Spirit, as though somehow, the Spirit can leak out of us. But there's a strong argument that here it is the Spirit who is doing the filling. Fullness has been a huge theme in Ephesians: the church displays the "fullness" of Christ (1:23), hence Paul's prayer for Christians to be filled with the "fullness of God" (3:19). Similarly, the goal of church has been "fullness of Christ" (4:13). It seems that Paul is showing it's the Spirit's work to mediate God's fullness in Christ, as we're transformed to live in a manner worthy of his plan.

Apply

- ❷ What activities can be a means by which the Spirit fills us with Christ, according to 5:19-20?
- ❷ How does understanding that these are the way the Spirit fills us change how you view these activities?

A word to the wives

Today we turn to the final thing that Paul flags up as being part of Spirit-fuelled living, in turn opening up a new section on how we order our relationships.

Spirit-fuelled submission

Read Ephesians 5:21

❓ *What comes to mind when you hear the word "submit"?*

The Greek word "submit" had clear overtones of authority, not in the sense of "giving orders" but of things being "in order".

Rather than advocating for mutual submission among all Christians, verse 21 seems best understood as a headline for the specific instances that will follow: "Submit to one another... and what I mean is..."

···· TIME OUT ··

❓ *How does our non-Christian culture tend to think of authority and submission? Why might this be?*

As with the church

These are controversial verses in our day. Let's listen carefully to what God's apostle says and what he doesn't say...

Read Ephesians 5:22-24

❓ *What are wives to do and who are they doing it for (v 22)?*
❓ *What is Paul's crucial theological rationale in verse 23?*
❓ *What isn't his rationale?*

Paul's use of "head" in Ephesians (1:22; 4:14) undoubtedly gives a clear sense of authority and leadership. As we look back at the church's relationship with Christ in Ephesians, we get a sense of "church-like" submission too. Ultimately, Christians "submit" by entrusting themselves to Christ's loving leadership and direction, which is not stifling but for our joy. As one writer says, "authority does not mean tyranny and submission does not mean inferiority".

⌄ Apply

We may feel Paul is infuriatingly brief here, but brevity can speak volumes. He doesn't call for unthinking obedience, or advocate for any cultural "feminine" stereotypes. Instead he addresses wives as those with a God-given role and responsibility, underlining that their submission comes from their will, not via a husband's demands.

❓ *Often people get stuck on the idea of God "writing headship and submission into the DNA of marriage". What difference does it make to see that primarily God has written Jesus' relationship with the church into the DNA of marriage?*
❓ *For wives, what makes submission hard? What makes it attractive? How can you look to Christ amidst the challenges?*
❓ *If you're a husband, how do you feel about having someone entrust themselves to you in this way?*

Sadly, the precious truths within these verses can be distorted to abuse women. If you or someone you know is in harm's way, please seek help immediately.

A word to the husbands

Sometimes the controversy surrounding Paul's words to wives means that we miss the shock of what he says to husbands…

That one little word
Read Ephesians 5:25-27

- ❓ *What "simple" command does Paul give husbands?*
- ❓ *Whose example should husbands follow—and what did this look like?*
- ❓ *Why do we have such a detailed description of Christ's love?*

Paul has already stated a husband is "head" of his wife (v 23), but strikingly this isn't repeated here. There's no excuse for husbands "ruling" over their wives. Instead we have a staggering description of Christ's sacrificial love—and the "simple" call to do likewise.

Love yourself?
Read Ephesians 5:28-30

- ❓ *How does Paul develop his point in verse 28? Does it remind you of any other Bible teaching?*
- ❓ *What might he be countering in verse 29?*

In verse 30, it's as if Paul has to pause and marvel at the privilege of receiving Christ's love. Is Paul resorting to "self-love" to motivate husbands here? Actually, the command to love "as yourself" was rooted in the Old Testament (Leviticus 19:18) and Jesus' teaching (Matthew 7:12). The rationale is not that husbands get something back, but that, given we're generally pretty good at looking after our own interests, we'd do well to apply this "loving" consideration to our wives!

This is about that
Read Ephesians 5:31-33

- ❓ *What is Paul quoting in verse 31? Why?*

A "mystery" (v 32) in Ephesians is not something strange but something now revealed.

- ❓ *What does Paul "reveal" about human marriage?*
- ❓ *How does verse 33 sum up the overall section on marriage?*

It's not that God looks at human marriage and decides to use it as a "real thing" illustration of his love for us. It's the other way around. Jesus' relationship with his bride is the "real thing"—and human marriage has been created by God to reflect and illustrate that "ultimate divine reality".

✔ Apply

If you're a husband (or hope to be a husband), do you think about headship as primarily a calling to love? Is this your priority?

- ❓ *How does seeing the "ultimate divine reality" behind human marriage help us if we're single and feeling like we're missing out?*
- ❓ *How can you look forward to your ultimate wedding day (see Revelation 21:1-4)?*
- ❓ *How might wives be able to encourage Christlikeness in their husbands?*

A song of ascents

Psalms 120 – 134 are all headed (NIV and ESV) "A song of ascents". Almost certainly this was a collection of songs to be sung by pilgrims as they went up to Jerusalem.

Read Psalm 122

❷ *What does Psalm 122 tell us about what Jerusalem was like at this time (v 1-5)?*
❷ *What happened there?*

In verses 1-5 it is as if the pilgrim stands on the edge of the city exclaiming in wonder at what he has found! When people first suggested going on pilgrimage, "I rejoiced" (v 1), most especially because they were going "to the house of the LORD". They would soon arrive at the temple, where sinners could come close to the living God without being burnt alive because their sins could be covered by sacrifice and forgiveness could be found.

⌄ Apply

The wonder that a true old-covenant believer would feel about the temple helps us with the awe and astonished delight we should feel about Jesus Christ. Every sensation of relieved joy felt by this believer can be amplified in your heart and mine as we meditate on sins forgiven by the sacrifice of Jesus, and access into the very presence of God the Father through the high-priestly mediation of Jesus.

Longing for Jerusalem

The Jerusalem celebrated in verses 1-5 was not fulfilled in the historical Jerusalem of Old Testament history. It was a Jerusalem seen only with the eyes of faith. It still is. It will not reach its fulfilment until Jesus Christ, who has died, has been raised and has ascended to heaven, builds his world-wide church and then returns from heaven to gather together his church to dwell in the perfect heavenly Jerusalem when it comes down from heaven to earth. It is that heavenly Jerusalem we see most clearly anticipated in the language of this psalm. And it is precisely because the reality fell so far short of the prophecies that the psalm ends as it does—with the exhortation to pray.

❷ *What does David urge people to pray for (v 6-9)?*

Just as verses 1-5 point to the heavenly Jerusalem to come, so verses 6-9 exhort us to pray for the church of Jesus Christ. We are to pray that the beautiful vision of verses 1-5 will be realised in the church. We are to pray that our local church will be a place where God is present in his forgiving grace, where men and women scarred by a dangerous world can find safety and where divided peoples see barriers fall as they bow together before the loving authority of Jesus Christ.

⌃ Pray

Pray these things for your own local church now. Pray that it will be the place your "family and friends" so badly need (v 8).

Lord of the family

Paul now turns to that most precious—and painful—relationship: parents and children! It's an area where we can often feel pressure and guilt, as well as ungodly aspirations.

Respect to the parents
Read Ephesians 6:1-3

The term for "children" wasn't bound by age, but it seems Paul is particularly thinking of those still being "brought up" (v 4).

- ❓ *What do you make of Paul addressing children directly?*
- ❓ *How is Paul's choice of words different to how he encourages wives (5:22)?*
- ❓ *What might this tell us?*
- ❓ *What difference does Paul adding "in the Lord" (6:1) make (see also 5:22; 6:5)?*

Paul quotes from the Ten Commandments (Deuteronomy 5:16; Exodus 20:12).

- ❓ *How does Paul reapply the fifth commandment in Ephesians 6:3?*

Obeying our parents "in the Lord" rules out following ungodly advice, instruction, or even aspirations. We are to do whatever Jesus wants us to do, in respect to our parents.

✅ Apply

- ❓ *What might it look like to "honour" your parents this week, however old you are?*
- ❓ *What difference does Jesus' lordship make to your relationship with your parents?*

Mercy for the kids
Read Ephesians 6:4

The word Paul uses for "fathers" (v 4) can be used for parents in general, but it is different to the word already used in verse 1, making it likely he now has fathers in view.

- ❓ *Why do you think Paul especially addresses fathers (see also 5:23)?*
- ❓ *What temptation does he think parents are most likely to struggle with?*
- ❓ *What would be the opposite?*
- ❓ *What does Paul expect to be happening in the Christian home (6:4)?*

✅ Apply

Parenting is exhausting work. The temptation to lose patience and be excessively severe, unreasonable or unfair comes easily.

- ❓ *If you're a parent, what situations tend to exasperate your children?*
- ❓ *Being honest, what influences your parenting most? How does seeing it within the context of God's eternal plan for the Lord Jesus bring perspective?*

It's worth noting that there are lots of great resources available to help with this responsibility—including older parents within our church families. Why not commit to making use of some?

✅ Pray

The challenges of being a Christian child and a Christian parent require daily grace! Pray for God's help for your own situation, and share your challenges with a friend.

Lord of work

For Christians, every area of life is an arena to be "filled" with Jesus' lordship. Paul now turns to first-century household slavery; even this can be an opportunity to live for Christ.

> ❓ *If you work, what's the thing about work that you find hardest as a Christian?*

Remember, Paul is still spelling out what it means to "submit to one another out of reverence for Christ" (5:21), as part of the Spirit's work of "filling us" with Christ (5:18). Thankfully most modern-day work-places are very different to slavery, yet the principles behind Paul's words still apply.

Audience of one

Read Ephesians 6:5-8

Just as with children and wives, Paul addresses slaves directly, which was highly unusual! Every Christian has a God-given dignity and calling to live for Christ, whether or not the prevailing culture values our role or status.

> ❓ *How would Paul's description of the slaves' masters as "earthly" have lifted their eyes (v 5)?*
> ❓ *What words and ideas are repeated?*
> ❓ *List the different motivations Paul gives. Do any surprise you? Why?*

⌄ Apply

> ❓ *If you are employed or carry out a service for clients, what different motivations do you find yourself struggling with?*

The impartial Master

The content of Paul's words to masters would probably have been more culturally shocking than his words to slaves.

Read Ephesians 6:9

> ❓ *Paul's comments to masters initially seem much briefer—but what do you notice about how Paul begins verse 9?*
> ❓ *What does this mean?*
> ❓ *What might Paul have in mind when he says "do not threaten them"?*
> ❓ *In a culture where masters had license to manipulate, abuse and exercise tyranny over their slaves, how might these verses have made Christian masters stand out?*

⌄ Apply

> ❓ *How does this passage demolish the idea of a sacred/secular divide?*
> ❓ *Jesus shows "no favouritism" So who should you treat differently at work?*
> ❓ *Imagine the tasks of the day ahead. What difference will it make to see every bit of your work as "serving the Lord" (v 7)?*

⌃ Pray

Talk to God about the day ahead. Where does this passage particularly convict you? How does it encourage you? Reflect upon our heavenly Lord's gaze. Each of us has a kind Master who sees everything and shows no favouritism to title, pay grade, or social status.

It's a battle

This is an especially well-known, often-quoted and much-loved Bible passage! But how does the "armour of God" fit within the rest of Ephesians?

Know your enemy

Read Ephesians 6:10-13

- ❷ *What is the overall command (v 10)?*
- ❷ *What should we expect the Christian life to feel like?*
- ❷ *Are we to summon up strength within ourselves? Why not?*
- ❷ *What role do 1:19-20 and 3:16, 20 play?*
- ❷ *Who are our opponents in this battle (v 11-12)?*

☑ Apply

Sometimes Christians might be tempted to identify our enemy as "culture" or particular unbelievers.

- ❷ *How does this passage correct this? How do they connect (see also 2:2)?*

···· TIME OUT ···

Read Isaiah 11:4-5; 49:2; 52:7; 59:17

- ❷ *Who seems to be wearing the armour in these passages?*
- ❷ *What difference does it make to know this armour has been worn by the Lord and his "Christ" as he saves his people?*

Wearing his armour

Having set out the need to put on the "full armour of God" (Ephesians 6:11, 13), Paul now spells it out...

Read Ephesians 6:14-18

- ❷ *What do you notice about this armour? Take a moment to trace the "armour" through Ephesians...*
  - *Belt of truth—see 1:13 and 4:15*
  - *Breastplate of righteousness—see 4:24*
  - *Feet of gospel of peace—see 2:14*
  - *Shield of faith—see 2:8*
  - *Helmet of salvation—see 1:13*
  - *Sword of the spirit—see 4:11*
- ❷ *In what sense do Christians already have the armour? So what might it mean to "put on" this armour?*
- ❷ *If putting on this armour means "putting on" what God has already done in his eternal plan, how does this re-emphasise our need for a "heart knowledge" (as in chapters 1 – 3)?*

It's striking that Paul repeatedly uses the language of "standing" (6:11, 13, 14). This isn't about fighting on our own, but standing by faith in the reality of Christ's completed work.

☑ Apply

- ❷ *How do you feel about having a spiritual enemy? Do you think you underplay this or over-worry about it?*
- ❷ *What difference does it make to know that the decisive victory has already been won by God through Christ?*
- ❷ *Do you seek to "arm yourself" with the gospel on a daily basis? Why not ask a Christian friend how they seek to do this?*

Fearless living; undying love

Congratulations—you've made it through this epic letter. And what a journey it's been: breathless and fast-paced, but always deep, profound and shaped by the gospel.

Fearless ministry

Paul has laid out the scope of God's eternal plan and then shown us what it means to "walk" in it. Now, having called us to be prayerful (v 18), Paul finally catches his breath and shares his own prayer request...

Read Ephesians 6:19-20

- ❓ *What is Paul's closing request?*
- ❓ *What is repeated?*
- ❓ *How does the detail of verse 20 remind us of Paul's circumstances (see also 3:1, 13)?*
- ❓ *What "fears" do you imagine Paul was tempted by? How has Ephesians engaged with these fears?*
- ❓ *How do these verses show how God's eternal plan is shaping Paul's priorities?*

Faithful partnership

Read Ephesians 6:21-22

Tychicus worked closely with Paul towards the end of his ministry (Acts 20:4; 2 Timothy 4:12; Titus 1:12) and probably delivered this letter for Paul (Ephesians 6:22). He may even have delivered Colossians on the very same journey, hence the reference to others hearing about Paul ("you also", v 21).

- ❓ *What do we learn about Tychicus from these verses?*
- ❓ *How will Tychicus' visit have been an example to the Ephesians of all that Paul has laid out?*

Undying love

Just like an email or a text message, it would have been normal for first-century letters to have a closing greeting. Paul typically used his sign-offs to pray for God's blessing, often known as a "benediction".

Read Ephesians 6:23-24 and 1:1-2, 15

- ❓ *How does Paul's ending mirror the way the letter began?*
- ❓ *Why are prayers for God's peace, love and grace a fitting way to end?*
- ❓ *How does Paul underline the need for a personal response in 6:24?*

🔽 Apply

Responding to Ephesians isn't about just getting our heads around a book. Neither is it simply about taking on board Paul's teaching. Ultimately, God calls for us to respond in love to "our Lord Jesus Christ" (v 24), as we are filled with a heart knowledge of God's eternal plan for Christ.

- ❓ *How has seeing God's eternal plan in Ephesians changed you?*
- ❓ *What are you particularly wanting to put into practice?*

🔼 Pray

Take some time to give thanks for all God has shown you in this precious book. Pray for your own "love" to grow, as Christ's love gets to work in your heart.

RUTH: The sojourn

This is a story with a dark and difficult beginning. In the first five verses of the book of Ruth, things just go from bad to worse.

Read Ruth 1:1-5

This story took place during the time in which "the judges ruled" (v 1). This was a period of spiritual darkness, when God's people repeatedly rebelled against him and were punished. Ruth zooms in on one particular family's trials and tragedies.

Elimelech's family

- ❓ *Who are the key characters in these verses? Try drawing a family tree.*
- ❓ *What goes wrong for this family to begin with (v 1)?*

We should read this situation with Deuteronomy in mind. God promised blessing on his people for obedience (Deuteronomy 28:1-14), but curses for disobedience—including famine (28:15-68). During the time of Ruth, this warning came true. The fields were barren and the crops failed.

But instead of mourning over the sin of the land and asking God to restore things, Elimelech left the fields of Bethlehem for Moab. This move was not like that of a person today migrating to another country. God had promised that his presence would dwell in Israel. So by moving away, Elimelech was turning his back on the Lord.

⌄ Apply

Elimelech's name means "My God is King". He did not listen to his own name. He made his decision without reference to God.

- ❓ *What upcoming decisions do you have?*
- ❓ *How can you make sure you go God's way rather than your own way?*

From bad to worse

- ❓ *What else goes wrong for Elimelech's family (Ruth 1:3, 5)?*
- ❓ *How do you imagine Naomi felt by the end of verse 5?*

Naomi did not know how things would turn out, but readers have the privilege of knowing her whole story. It is a story that will go from emptiness to fullness, from tragedy to glory. It shows us that God is still trustworthy in the midst of emptiness and difficulty. The question for us is: can we bring ourselves to trust him when we suffer?

In these verses there is just a tiny hint at the future that God has prepared for Naomi. She comes from Bethlehem, which of course is associated with David and ultimately the birth of Jesus. It is actually from Naomi's insignificant family, in an insignificant little town, that the Saviour of the world, the King of kings, would come.

⌃ Pray

Spend some time praising God for the way that he works through all things—including disasters and darkness, and every apparently insignificant detail of our lives.

Road to return

Looking back over our lives, we can often see significant moments, where change occurs. What key turning points have you faced in your life?

In today's passage there is a geographical and a spiritual turning point. It is about turning back to Bethlehem, and also about turning back to the Lord in faith.

Read Ruth 1:6-10

Verse 6 contains many hints about the nature of the wonderful provision of our God. He allowed Naomi to *hear* the news from Israel; he came compassionately to *visit* those suffering in famine; he came to his people, with whom he had made a covenant; and he did not overlook their basic needs but gave them food. This was the context in which Naomi, Ruth, and Orpah had to decide what to do next.

The decision

- ❷ What does Naomi tell Ruth and Orpah to do?
- ❷ What is her hope for them?
- ❷ What is her view of God?

The word "kindness" is the rich Hebrew word *hesed*, which refers to God's loyalty, faithfulness, grace, mercy and compassion. Naomi believes that God is indeed kind, and that his power and grace extend beyond the borders of Israel.

Naomi compares the way Ruth and Orpah have treated her with the way she hopes God may treat them (v 8). These daughters-in-law have been compassionate to Naomi, and so she longs for them to be richly blessed. Specifically, she prays for them to be settled and secure, and for the Lord to bless them both with another husband.

- ❷ What words would you use to describe Ruth and Orpah's response (v 9-10)?

⌃ Pray

- ❷ Who do you know who reflects the kindness of God? Praise God for them and pray for them. Consider sending a message to thank them.
- ❷ Can you think of times when God has dealt kindly with you? Praise him for this.
- ❷ Do you ever find it hard to think of God as kind? Why? Ask him for his help with this.

Your people

One theme in the Bible that is often overlooked, especially in individualistic cultures, is the concept of community. Yet it is a theme woven throughout the Bible. God displays his glory to and through his people: we are saved into a community.

Ruth and Orpah express a desire not only to go with their mother-in-law but to go to her people (v 10)—severing ties with the Moabites. This idea was extraordinary in the ancient world. It hints at the possibility of conversion. They have a chance to become part of God's people.

Three pictures of church

Psalms 126 – 128 each speak of Zion as a project in some way. They shed great light for us on the work of the gospel in building local churches.

The church of Christ is the most deeply wonderful project in the world. There is no higher cause to which we can devote our love and our energies. These three psalms will help us to consider what that means for each of us in our local church.

A harvest sown in tears

Read Psalm 126

> ❷ *Why is the psalmist rejoicing?*
> ❷ *What does he plead for?*

The psalm depicts a world in which people care more for Zion than for their individual prosperity. So in new-covenant terms, the psalm is the expression of a heart that cares more deeply and passionately about the cause of Christ and the church of Christ than it does for its own success, comfort, good name or health.

So let us pray that we would sing or speak these words today in their new-covenant meaning. As we do so, we will find welling up in our hearts such a deep delight in the prosperity of the church of Christ, expressed in our own local church, that it overwhelms all our personal joys or cares.

⌃ Pray

When the waters come to a desert area such as the Negev (v 4), buried seeds that have lain dormant for a long time suddenly germinate and sprout. Ask God to do this for your church, crying to the Lord for the watering of his Spirit that alone can give new life.

God is the builder

Read Psalm 127

> ❷ *What does the psalmist say is in vain?*
> ❷ *How does he describe children?*

In Psalm 127, the picture starts with a city being built, then moves to a family. We see that the true builder is the Lord himself. Unless God is at work, nothing will happen. It is all in vain (v 1-2). Then the picture moves on from building the city to the need for it to be populated (v 3-5).

A family from God

Read Psalm 128

> ❷ *What is the route to blessing?*
> ❷ *How are children described this time, and how does this differ from Psalm 127?*

Psalm 128 continues the family image from Psalm 127. This is not about our nuclear-family hopes; this is the growth of the people of God, and ultimately the church of Jesus Christ. And there is a sense in which this God-fearing man, both in 127:3-5 and throughout Psalm 128, is fulfilled in Jesus Christ himself, to whom is given many, many spiritual children, who will be made like him and who will populate the new Jerusalem.

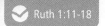

Your God, my God

When did you first profess faith? What led you to that decision?

Today's passage gives us a portrait of a conversion—and of faith that's worth imitating.

Read Ruth 1:11-14

Naomi's opinion is firm. She advises her daughters-in-law to turn back.

It was customary for a childless widow to marry her husband's brother in order to raise children and continue the dead husband's line. But Naomi's two dead sons have no brothers, so there is no hope of that happening. Since her family line cannot continue, she wants Ruth and Orpah to remarry and start new families.

> ❓ *How does Naomi describe what has happened to her family (v 13)?*
> ❓ *Who does she see as the main victim?*

Naomi blames God and doesn't have much hope for the future. But she does at least see God's involvement in her life. She knows that things are not outside of God's sovereign control.

Orpah kisses her mother-in-law goodbye. But Ruth clings to her tightly.

Risk-taking faith

Read Ruth 1:15-18

Orpah's decision makes sense on a practical level, but Ruth's decision is based on active faith.

> ❓ *In what ways does Ruth express faith here?*

> ❓ *Who and what does she commit to?*

In Hebrew poetic structure, the sentence or word that comes in the middle is often the most important. Here, verses 16a and 17 frame Ruth's glorious profession of faith: "Your people shall be my people, and your God my God".

Ruth's declaration is not primarily about her commitment to Naomi. It is about her commitment to the Lord.

✔ Apply

> ❓ *Do you think your faith is more like Naomi's or more like Ruth's? Or do you struggle to have faith at all?*
> ❓ *How could you show faith like Ruth's, practically speaking? You could ask someone to pray with you about this.*

⌃ Pray

Ruth had lived with Naomi for ten years. While Naomi does not appear to have been a winsome witness, it is clear that somewhere along the way Ruth heard of and believed in the God of Israel, by his grace.

We must pray that God would use us to lead more "Ruths" to faith. Pray that you may "walk in wisdom toward outsiders," speaking winsome and gracious words, and that he would use you to bear witness (Colossians 4:2-6).

The arrival

Naomi has had some terrible losses—but also some very good news. Now she is back in Bethlehem where she started. How will she describe her journey so far?

Read Ruth 1:19-22

❷ *Why do you think the women say, "Is this Naomi?" (v 19)?*

❷ *How does Naomi describe herself?*

"Naomi" means "pleasant" and "Mara" means "bitter". Naomi believes her situation demands a new name—one that reflects her frustration.

TIME OUT

The name "Mara" has a noteworthy history. When God's people rebelled in the wilderness, complaining about a lack of provision, Marah was the name of the place where they grumbled against him (Exodus 15:22-25). They could not drink the bitter water, so they cried out to the Lord and he made it drinkable and sweet. Naomi reflects the heart of her ancestors: she complains about her situation, failing to see the grace of God in her life (expressed in part by the daughter-in-law who stands beside her). We wonder if the bitter one will ever become sweet again.

Can I vent?

Naomi is having a venting session. Maybe it will help things! She attributes her pain to God; strikingly, there is no acknowledgment of personal accountability. She also forgets that it is part of God's character to care for widows (Exodus 22:22-23; Psalm 68:5; 146:9).

❷ *What four things does Naomi say the LORD has done to her?*

⌃ Pray

Do you know anyone who might describe their situation the way Naomi does? Psalm 146 talks about how God helps the oppressed and needy. Look it up and use it to help you to pray for them.

Another return

There are some similarities between Naomi's return and the story of the prodigal son (Luke 15:11-32). In rebellion, the son turns his back on his father and leaves for a far country, where he squanders his money. Then there is a famine and the son is so hungry that he longs to eat pig food. Eventually he wakes up to the reality that in his father's house there is "more than enough bread" (v 17)—and he returns.

Unlike the prodigal son, Naomi does not return broken and contrite. She expresses bitterness instead of brokenness. However, Naomi is also returning home at the prospect of bread. She comes back at the beginning of the barley harvest in Bethlehem—which literally means "house of bread". There is a new beginning agriculturally. Will there be a new beginning in other ways for these women—as there was for the prodigal son?

Introducing Boaz

Keep your eye on this guy! In Ruth 2 we meet a "worthy man"—someone of wealth and integrity.

Throughout the rest of the book we will see that Boaz is a model of integrity, compassion, and justice. But he is also a picture of Christ. Boaz's grace points to Jesus' grace–the grace that has bought our salvation, and the grace that strengthens and empowers us to love this broken world. Look carefully at the way Boaz treats Ruth, because it is also the way Jesus has treated us.

The field

Read Ruth 2:1-3

Boaz is a relative of Naomi's husband—"of the clan of Elimelech" (v 1, 3). This detail will become significant later!

> ❷ *What is Ruth's hope as she goes out to glean?*
> ❷ *How does she end up in Boaz's field?*

Gleaning consisted of gathering leftover grain. God's law commanded harvesters to leave the edges of the field for the poor and not retrieve dropped crops (Deuteronomy 24:19-22; Leviticus 19:9-10). This was a way to help the poor survive—though it still required effort and work on their part.

Ruth goes to the fields with a sense of humility. She recognizes her need for favour. She illustrates the proverb "Toward the scorners [God] is scornful, but to the humble he gives favour" (Proverbs 3:34) and the words of James: "God opposes the proud but gives grace to the humble" (James 4:6).

Perfect timing

Read Ruth 2:4-7

There is a note of wonder in the word "Behold," preparing us to hear that Boaz has arrived—just at the right time.

> ❷ *What is our first impression of Boaz (v 4)?*
> ❷ *What impression does he gain of Ruth (v 6-7)?*

Apply

Ruth is dependent on others' favour, yet she does not wait around for help. She tries to make the very best of her situation that she can, working hard and trusting God to be good to her as she does so.

Meanwhile, Boaz's faith is expressed in an everyday greeting. He has the Lord on his mind in the ordinary routine of life.

> ❷ *Is there anything that you are waiting for the Lord to do? Do you need to trust him more? Do you need to work hard and take steps yourself?*
> ❷ *How could you keep God in mind during your everyday life?*
> ❷ *How could you use your words to build up and bless others each day this week?*

Faith and favour

Have you ever felt totally overwhelmed by someone else's kindness? That's how Ruth feels in today's passage.

Read Ruth 2:8-13

Boaz is determined to provide for Ruth. He does not only tell her that she may glean in his field but actually insists that she stay there (v 8-9).

> ❓ *How else does Boaz show favour to Ruth in verses 8-9?*
> ❓ *Why is Ruth so surprised at this (v 10)?*

In addition to food provision, Boaz goes on to show favour to Ruth in another way. He blesses her with his words. You can imagine what the affirmation of a godly, influential leader must have sounded like to her.

> ❓ *What does Boaz praise Ruth for (v 11)?*

Boaz believes that what Ruth has done is a result of her faith in God. It is the Lord whom she has pleased by her actions (v 12).

> ❓ *What image does Boaz use to describe Ruth's faith?*
> ❓ *Does this image feel like a good description of your own relationship with God? Why, or why not?*

TIME OUT

The psalmists also use the image of wings to express trust in the Lord (Psalm 17:8; 36:7; 91:1-4). A similar image is used by Jesus when he weeps over Jerusalem, saying that he longs to gather them as "a hen gathers her brood under her wings" (Matthew 23:37). How sad it is that people reject Christ's salvation and his rest!

Pause now to thank God for his rescue and protection. You may want to ask him to make this sense of refuge and safety more real to you. Ask for his help in telling the world where to go to find this eternal grace.

Mercy and justice

> ❓ *How does Ruth summarise what Boaz has done for her (Ruth 2:13)?*

Boaz provides for the hungry—following God's word regarding the widow, the stranger, and the poor. He also protects Ruth, charging the men not to harm her. He uses his influence for those who have no influence. And he uses his words to bless Ruth, showing her personal dignity and respect.

Boaz exemplifies mercy, justice, and the grace and favour which God shows to his people. He is an example of Micah 6:8:

"What does the Lord require of you but to do justice, and to love kindness, and to walk humbly with your God?"

Pray

Pray for those in your community who are in need of provision, protection, or dignity.

Pray for yourself and those who are close to you. Ask God to show you how to do justice, love kindness and walk humbly with him.

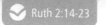
Roasted grain

We might like to think of today's passage as Boaz and Ruth's first date. But it is not a romantic evening meal—more like a lunch break at work.

Even so, Boaz's hospitality is gracious and exemplary.

Read Ruth 2:14-18

> ❷ *How does Boaz continue to welcome Ruth?*
> ❷ *How does he go above and beyond his duty?*

As a result of Boaz's kindness, Ruth gathers an abundance: a whole ephah of barley. That's some 30 pounds (13.6kg) of food—several weeks' worth. Ruth apparently hauls this back to Naomi's place all by herself. This Moabite can carry some grain!

☑ Apply

Ruth shows the same kindness to Naomi that Boaz has shown to her. Her example is challenging.

Do you find it hard to love bitter people and to serve difficult people? If so, then allow Ruth to instruct and inspire you! Love the "Naomis" in your life in the way that Christ has shown love to you.

> ❷ *Who do you find difficult to love?*
> ❷ *What could you do to love and serve them today?*

Hope for the future

Read Ruth 2:19-23

> ❷ *Who does Naomi bless (v 19, 20)? Why?*

Naomi seems to be saying that the Lord is showing kindness to her whole family—to her and to Ruth, both women with deceased husbands. But how can the Lord show kindness to the dead?

Boaz is a kinsman-redeemer (v 20). The law instructed that when a man died, his brother was obliged to marry his widow and raise his children. He was even to give the dead man's name to the first child born out of the new marriage. This would ensure that the inheritance would continue to be associated with the dead relative. If Boaz is willing to act as a redeemer for Naomi's family, he can marry Ruth and continue the family line of Elimelech.

> ❷ *What other reasons are there for Ruth to stay in Boaz's field (v 21-22)?*

Ruth and Naomi are vulnerable widows in a patriarchal society. They need provision now and security for the future. They cannot solve this problem on their own: they need a redeemer. A husband and a child for Ruth will end the crisis, provide for their needs, and continue the family line.

⌃ Pray

Think of anyone you know who seems to be in a hopeless situation. Pray that God will bless them and not forsake them.

Thank God for the hope that he has given you for the future, and the eternal security that you have in Christ. Ask for strength to share this hope with others.

 Bible in a year: 1 Chronicles 7-9 • Luke 1:21-38

At the threshing floor

Chapter 2 left us hanging. Will anything happen between Ruth and Boaz?

Naomi is determined to ensure something does happen between them.

The plan
Read Ruth 3:1-5

> ❷ *What is Naomi's hope for Ruth (v 1-2)?*
> ❷ *What are the steps of Naomi's plan?*

The threshing floor was the place where farmers would get rid of the chaff—the unwanted husk around the kernel of grain—by tossing the harvested grain into the air with a pitchfork. This was done at night because night breezes were needed to blow the chaff away. Naomi sees an opportunity for Ruth.

Ruth is to uncover Boaz's feet and lie down close to him. The purpose of such a sensual gesture is intended to communicate something to Boaz. Apparently it was a customary means of requesting marriage.

This is a risky plan. Boaz could respond harshly or accuse Ruth of acting like a prostitute. He could easily assault her if he wanted to. As Naomi gives these instructions and Ruth wholeheartedly accepts them, they are both displaying enormous trust in Boaz. The plan all depends upon his integrity.

☑ Apply

The same is true for us as Christian believers. We can take risks for Jesus because we know we can depend on his kindness, integrity, and redeeming power.

> ❷ *What risks are you afraid of taking for Christ? Write down something you will do this week to step out in faith.*

The proposal
Read Ruth 3:6-9

> ❷ *How is Boaz's shock and confusion communicated (v 8-9)?*
> ❷ *What does Ruth ask Boaz to do?*

"Spread your wings" (or "garment") is elsewhere an idiom for marriage (see Ezekiel 16:8). It is also the image Boaz used to describe how Ruth sought refuge in God (Ruth 2:12). Now Ruth is asking Boaz to become part of God's protection and provision for her life.

Boaz is "a redeemer", not "the redeemer". Naomi has other male relatives, so Boaz is not obliged to marry Ruth. But Ruth knows he is willing to follow the spirit of the law, not just its minimum requirements.

☑ Pray

Reflect on Jesus' character and ask for his help in trusting him. Pray for friends who find it hard to trust Jesus. You could send them a message reminding them of his trustworthiness.

By the rivers

We do not know when Psalm 137 was first written and sung. But it bears the marks of eye-witness memory, of one who knew what it was to be an exile in Babylon.

Read Psalm 137

- ❓ *Why can't God's people sing (v 1-4)?*
- ❓ *Why did their captors demand a song?*
- ❓ *What curse does the psalmist (a musician) call upon himself if he forgets Zion (v 5-6)?*

For the believers in exile, the songs of Zion appear absurd—as wishful thinking. It is the same today, for we too are "exiles, scattered" (1 Peter 1:1). We look at the reality of the church of Jesus Christ, and it is very hard to sing about the glories of that church as they are promised in the word of God. It is very tempting to hang up our harps and to abandon all attempts at gospel proclamation.

Apply

- ❓ *When are you tempted to look at your local church like this?*
- ❓ *What impact does this have on your own gospel proclamation?*

The singer in Psalm 137:5 believes the promises about Zion even when there is nothing to show for them. He counts them more precious than gold. *Babylon is visible, audible, delightful, and all around me,* he sings; *but I rest my joy on the promises of God.*

Apply

The church, the bride of Jesus, has a destiny far brighter than the shiniest wonders of "Babylon" today. We haven't yet seen the bride (the church) in her glory, but we know that one day she will shine in glorious robes (see Revelation 19:7-8)—while Babylon ceases to look like anything at all (Revelation 18:1-3, 21-24).

- ❓ *What difference will it make to your life if you reckon on this promise being true?*

The focus in Psalm 137:7-9 is on the enemies whose hostility took God's people into exile: Edom and Babylon. Verse 9 is horrifying. But it is necessary (see the discussion of Psalm 109 on day 18). It is not a curse but a declaration of something that is true. One day Babylon will be no more. It is chilling; but it is necessary. If the children of Babylon live, then Babylon lives and will rise again. But the day will come when Babylon will not rise again. We see this final defeat most clearly in Revelation 18:21-24 with its assuring refrain "never ... again". One day evil will be no more. One day hostility to God and his people will be no more.

Apply

This is a wonderful hope. It is sobering, for God's coming judgment will be terrible—and final. But it is necessary and good. Judgment is not something to be embarrassed about; it is a sober truth to make us glad and to strengthen our resolve to keep telling people the only gospel that offers rescue from that judgment.

The answer

What will Boaz say? Will he marry Ruth?

Read Ruth 3:10-13

It turns out that Boaz is not put off by Ruth's directness but pleased by it.

> ❷ *What is his initial response (v 10)?*

It seems safe to assume that Ruth is younger than Boaz. She could have gone after young men (literally, "choice men"), but decided not to pursue a guy out of greed, nor out of passion. Instead she has other values, such as family loyalty.

Stepping back for a moment, we are left to marvel at the purity of both Boaz and Ruth. Instead of engaging in some steamy sexual encounter, Boaz praises God for Ruth! Nor does Ruth make any sexual advances towards Boaz in an effort to win him.

We can imagine how fast Ruth's heart must have been beating—but Boaz comforts her by saying "Do not fear" (v 11).

> ❷ *What does Boaz promise to do (v 13)?*
> ❷ *Why (v 11, 12)?*

Provision

Read Ruth 3:14-18

Before it is light enough for people to recognise Ruth, Boaz sends her home. This is meant to preserve her dignity and reputation.

> ❷ *How else does Boaz care for Ruth (v 15)?*

The gift of grain is not only a provision of food. It is a message to Naomi. Boaz is serious about his pursuit of Ruth—so serious that this will involve caring for her mother-in-law too.

Naomi once described herself as "empty" (1:21), but now she has a full load of grain before her. We are witnessing her journey from emptiness to fullness, through the actions of Ruth and Boaz.

⌄ Apply

How similar Boaz's treatment of Ruth is to the way the Lord Jesus has dealt with us! We can be like Ruth, going to him respectfully but boldly to ask him to "spread [his] wings over us" and redeem us. He has made a promise that all who call on his name will become part of his bride, the church (Romans 10:9; Ephesians 5:28-33). And he has given us the most wonderful provision: the Holy Spirit who dwells in us. The Spirit is the "firstfruits" which promises more to come, assuring us of "the redemption of our bodies" (Romans 8:23).

> ❷ *What rescue or provision are you desperate for in your life or ministry?*
> ❷ *Are there things you particularly long for the Holy Spirit to do in and through you?*

Spend some time bringing these things to God, and praising him for his abundant and gracious provision.

Bible in a year: 1 Chronicles 16-18 • Luke 2:1-24

Looking through Boaz

Before we reach the final chapter of Ruth, it is worth pausing to understand more about the concept of redemption in the Bible.

In Old Testament law, a redeemer was someone who protected and helped his relatives.

Read Leviticus 25:25-28, 47-49

- ❓ *Who or what can be "redeemed" in these verses?*
- ❓ *Why is redemption necessary?*
- ❓ *Who can be a redeemer?*
- ❓ *What is the result of redemption for the person who is being helped?*

The story of God's people also reveals the fact that God himself is a redeemer. In the exodus, the people of Israel were enslaved in Egypt. They were desperate and in great need. So God promised redemption.

Read Exodus 6:6-7

- ❓ *Why is redemption needed here?*
- ❓ *What will God do to redeem his people?*
- ❓ *What is the result of redemption for the Israelites?*

Our Redeemer

The New Testament is clear that all of us are spiritually helpless and in need of redemption. But God "has rescued us from the dominion of darkness and brought us into the kingdom of the Son he loves, in whom we have redemption, the forgiveness of sins" (Colossians 1:13-14).

Redemption always has a price. In the Old Testament laws, it happened through a commercial transaction: a kinsman had to make a payment to redeem property and slaves. In the exodus, the payment for deliverance from Egypt was the sacrifice of a precious lamb at Passover.

Read Ephesians 2:12-13, 19-22

- ❓ *In what ways were we in the same position as Ruth (v 12)?*
- ❓ *But what price has been paid (v 13)?*
- ❓ *And what is the result?*

To be a redeemer you had to have both the willingness and the ability to redeem. When it came to Ruth's redemption, Boaz had both. He demonstrated the character of a redeemer through his selfless actions, and his status as a landowner meant he had the financial capacity to become a redeemer.

Only Jesus had the immeasurable worth necessary to redeem sinners. And he was willing: he was full of kindness and grace. He has made us part of his family, just like Old Testament redeemers, and just like the Israelites in the time of the exodus.

When we look at Boaz, we see many godly traits to imitate. But when we look through Boaz, we see the gospel of Jesus Christ.

⌃ Pray

Psalm 107 contains more examples of redemption. Use this psalm to help you "ponder the loving deeds of the LORD" (v 43)—including the redemption you have in Christ.

Bible in a year: 1 Chronicles 19-21 • Luke 2:25-52

Two redeemers

All eyes are on Boaz as he goes to make good his promise to Ruth.

There is another possible redeemer for Ruth and Naomi—a closer relative than Boaz. Boaz goes to find him.

At the city gate

Read Ruth 4:1-4

Legal transactions, judicial proceedings, and official business were all conducted at the city gate. It was also the best place to find someone: everyone in the city regularly passed through this gate. So Boaz sits here to wait for the other potential redeemer to come through.

❓ *How does he explain the situation to the other redeemer (v 3)?*

❓ *What next steps does he suggest (v 4)?*

❓ *How does the other redeemer respond?*

The land in question is all of Elimelech's property that had not been sold when the family made the journey to Moab (v 9). It was probably all that Naomi had. Presumably it was due to the desperate situation of herself and Ruth that Naomi needed to sell it.

Raising this issue of Naomi's property may be a way for Boaz to divert attention away from Ruth, in order to win her for himself. Or perhaps this is simply the most straightforward way of introducing the matter. Whichever, it is clear that redeeming Ruth and buying Naomi's land go together—as Boaz reveals next.

The true cost

Read Ruth 4:5-6

❓ *Why does the other redeemer change his mind?*

Redeeming the property would involve sacrifice. Redeeming Ruth by marriage as well as buying the field would require resolve and even the risk of losing a good reputation (since, as Boaz emphasises, Ruth is a Moabite).

This was not the only cost. When a widow was redeemed, the first son born in the new marriage would be recognised as the son of the woman's first husband, inheriting his property when he grew up and so perpetuating the name of the dead in his land (Deuteronomy 25:5). So if the other redeemer had a child with Ruth, he would eventually lose the field he had bought.

He is more concerned with his own welfare, property, and posterity than with the welfare of his relative, Naomi. By contrast, a true redeemer is willing to pay a price for the good of others.

⌃ Pray

Reflect on the cost of your own redemption. Spend some time praising God for Jesus.

What price may you need to pay to serve Christ and others? Pray that God will give you the willingness to do so.

Sealing the deal

The matter is settled. Boaz is the only one willing and able to pay the price.

Read Ruth 4:7-10

Boaz's "purchase" is confirmed through an ancient custom: removing a sandal.

With the official business complete, Boaz offers a speech—bookending it with the phrase "You are witnesses," just in case any future questions arise concerning the transaction.

But one more significant thing happens at the city gate.

A prayer of blessing

Read Ruth 4:11-12

- ❓ *What is the people's prayer for Ruth?*
- ❓ *What is their prayer for Boaz?*
- ❓ *What is their prayer for the family as a whole?*

Rachel and Leah were the wives of Jacob. Together with their two servants, Bilhah and Zilpah, they bore twelve sons whose descendants made up the twelve tribes of Israel (Genesis 29 – 30; 35:16-18). The people, then, are asking the Lord to give Ruth a place alongside these mothers of the people of God: that is, that she may be given a key role among God's people.

Tamar was the widow of Judah's son. She was childless, with no prospect of marrying again. So Tamar disguised herself as a prostitute, deceiving her own father-in-law, so that she might have a child by him (Genesis 38). Like Ruth, Tamar went out in active pursuit of a child and a better future.

Of course, Tamar and Judah's conduct was a lot less admirable than Ruth and Boaz's! But their union proved to play an important role in salvation history. God promised that the Messiah would come through Judah (Genesis 49:10), and Judah's strongest son was Perez, the son of Tamar.

The prayers of the people in Bethlehem were answered. Ruth did become a key person in the story of redemptive history. Boaz's family did have renown in Bethlehem. In fact, it was through Boaz's line that Israel's greatest king would come—King David (as we'll see at the end of the chapter).

⌃ Pray

You might not use the same examples as the people of Bethlehem, but it can be helpful to use Bible characters and Bible phrases to inform your prayers.

Choose a family you know. Consider the character traits of Ruth and Boaz—the way they are described and the way they act—and ask God to make the members of this family like that. Ask God to build his church through them and make them fruitful.

The end (almost)

The final section of Ruth reveals the staggering providence of God.

A son for Ruth and Boaz

Read Ruth 4:13

Saying that Boaz "took Ruth" is to say that "he took her home," an expression for marriage. Adding "and she became his wife" seems redundant—it is saying the same thing a second time—but its inclusion emphasizes Ruth's new status. She has repeatedly been "the Moabite" and "the foreigner", lower than a servant (e.g. 2:10, 13). But here in chapter 4 she is Ruth, the wife of Boaz. She has a brand new status, thanks to the sovereign grace of God.

The two of them go from wedding to baby in one verse! Fertility has been an issue all the way through the story—both the infertility of the land and the problem of childlessness. Both these needs have now been met. The narrator only explicitly mentions the Lord's involvement twice: once regarding his provision of food (1:6) and now with his provision of a son (4:13).

A redeemer for Naomi

Read Ruth 4:14-17

- ❓ *What phrases do the women use to describe the child?*
- ❓ *Who else do they praise (v 14, 17)?*

Surprisingly, it is not Boaz who is called a redeemer here but his son. This child will bless Naomi personally and continue her family line. How can we be sure of this?

The women point to his mother: he will be like her.

Ruth's devotion to Naomi is so great that having her is better than having seven sons. Seven was a number of perfection and sons were highly prized; and it was the loss of her sons that was a key reason for Naomi's bitterness in chapter 1. This expression is the ultimate tribute to Ruth's amazing life and loyalty.

- ❓ *Compare this passage with 1:1-5. How have the calamities at the beginning of the book been solved?*
- ❓ *Compare this passage with 1:19-21. How has Naomi's personal situation been transformed?*

Pray

- ❓ *In what ways has God worked throughout the story of Ruth?*
- ❓ *What surprises you about this?*
- ❓ *What comforts you?*

As you reflect on these things, spend some time worshipping God. Pray for anyone you know who is struggling at the moment—that they might know the extraordinary provision and care of the God who has redeemed them. Ask God to show you how he can use you, like Ruth, to bring fullness to those who are empty.

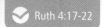
Good news genealogy

Don't rush over the genealogy at the end of Ruth. It's a vital glimpse of the bigger story.

A king for Israel

Read Ruth 4:17-22

Ruth is not just a story about two desperate widows—it is also about a desperate nation "in the days when the judges ruled" (1:1). Israel was broken by immorality and disunity. Obed would be the grandfather of David, the king who would give God's people leadership, unity, and security.

The ten names in 4:18-22 display God's answer to the prayer that Boaz and his line may be renowned in Bethlehem. Perez heads the royal line of Judah, which continues through a host of others to Boaz, Obed, Jesse, and finally David. The list is not exhaustive—there would have been other generations in between the names we read here (see 1 Chronicles 2). But it is meant to show the continuation of the line.

The future Messiah

David was Israel's most celebrated king. But more important than his military success was the promise that he was the paradigm for the future Messiah. God promised that one of David's sons would sit on the throne forever (2 Samuel 7:12b-16; Psalm 132:12). This comes to fulfilment in Jesus.

Read Matthew 1:1-17

Matthew's genealogy shows that Jesus has always been part of God's plans. It also shows that Ruth's story is not unique—God repeatedly incorporates unexpected and unworthy individuals into his people.

> ❷ *Pick out any names you recognize. What stories lie behind these names?*

Read Matthew 1:18-25

> ❷ *Look at how Jesus is described. In what ways is he like Obed, Boaz, and Ruth?*
> ❷ *In what ways is he better and greater than them?*

Think of the way in which Naomi and Ruth received provision from God. Were they just handed money? No! They experienced extraordinary kindness. The story ends with the picture of Naomi holding a child in her arms, having found real rest, peace, and intimacy.

For Christians there is an even greater resolution. Jesus is "God with us." By placing our faith in him, we find ultimate refuge, ultimate rest, and ultimate peace—in part now, and one day in full.

☑ Apply

Reflecting on the story of Ruth...

> ❷ *What would you say to someone who thinks they're not the right kind of person to be a Christian?*
> ❷ *What would you say to someone who is finding it hard to trust God's plans?*
> ❷ *What would you say to someone who feels far away from God's loving care?*

Search me, O Lord

Parts of this psalm are great favourites; they appear on devotional calendars and Instagram pics, and we love them. But there are two parts we are apt to omit.

First, we tremble when we reach verses 19-22, and we wish they weren't there. And we also forget that it is headed "Of David". We need to remember that this was first a psalm of David—and therefore also later a psalm of Jesus; and we must understand how it was sung by the King before it can be sung by us, as men and women united to the King by faith. As we shall see, that will help us know how to sing verses 19-22.

Read Psalm 139

❓ *What does David know about God?*
❓ *What does he know about himself?*
❓ *What does he know about his enemies?*

Verses 1-6 are not simply about the truth that God knows all things. God does not just know *about* the king, but knows *him*. Verses 7-12 are, likewise, about God's personal presence. David is not simply saying that he cannot find any place in the universe where God is not; he is saying that he cannot find any place in the universe where God is not *with him*.

❓ *Consider what a comfort verses 7-12 must have been to Jesus, when he sang this psalm as God's ultimate King.*

Creative wisdom

❓ *How many creative words can you find in verses 13-18?*

Now read verses 13-18 again, imagining Jesus being knit together in Mary's womb.

This knitting-together was the greatest miracle in human history. Jesus of Nazareth was shaped and prepared lovingly by the Father; he was the incarnate Son of God, who would work the Father's will in every way. Every day and night of the life of Jesus on earth was written in the Father's book before it came to be. What infinite skill and what amazing wisdom must have been expended in the shaping of Jesus, the incarnate Word!

And yet—and again this is an astonishing truth—in Christ each man and woman may say of themselves, "I too am God's personal loving handiwork; I too have been created by God, in Christ Jesus, so that I may do precisely the good works God has prepared in advance for me to do" (Ephesians 2:10).

The king's enemies

Since the psalmist is God's king, God's enemies are his enemies. Only on the lips of the king—ultimately the perfect King, Jesus—can verses 19-22 possibly be prayed. For Jesus is God's beloved and loving Son, and his appointed King—and therefore hostility to Jesus is enmity towards the Father.

⌃ Pray

In the final two verses, the king leads his people in prayer. So Jesus leads us to open ourselves afresh to the God who searches and knows us (v 1), that he may again search and know us (v 23).

Bible in a year: 2 Chronicles 4-6 • Luke 5:17-39

ROMANS: Right with God

Have you ever had a big name speaker come visit your church? Were you pleased to hear that they were coming?

Paul planned to visit the church in Rome on his way to Spain (verse 10, see also 15:24). The problem is that, everywhere Paul went, trouble followed close behind. Things don't quite go to plan and Paul eventually comes to Rome under guard (Acts 28:16).

What made Paul so controversial was his claim that both Jews and Gentiles (non-Jews) could be right with God through faith in Jesus without first having to meet some criteria (like being circumcised). In this letter Paul tackles this controversy head on.

Good news

Read Romans 1:1-4

The word "gospel" means "good news". The Christian message is an announcement of good news.

> ❓ *How does Paul describe this good news?*

The gospel is taught in "the Holy Scriptures" and it is all about Jesus. It's not something Paul has made up. In this letter Paul is going to show how the story of the Old Testament reaches its fulfilment in Jesus. Making people right with God through Jesus was always God's plan.

"Appointed the Son of God" (NIV) doesn't mean Jesus became God at his resurrection, for Jesus is the eternally begotten Son of God. Instead it means he was "declared" (ESV) to be the Son of God. Jesus was condemned to death as a blasphemer, but God vindicated his divine claims by raising him from the dead.

⌄ Apply

Telling people about your church is a great way to begin sharing the gospel. But the gospel is not the message of what your church has done. It's the message of what Jesus has done. So see if you can move the conversation on to Jesus.

Good news for everyone

Read Romans 1:5-7

> ❓ *What are the implications of this gospel for those who hear it?*
> ❓ *What are the implications of this gospel for Paul?*

"The obedience that comes from faith" could mean an obedient life that flows from faith or the obedient response which is faith. Either way, faith is key (as verse 17 will reiterate). The gospel calls us to repent of our self-rule and turn in faith to Christ. And this good news is a message we need to share with people from every nation.

> ❓ *How are you involved in taking the gospel to the nations? Going? Giving? Sending? Supporting? Praying?*

Not ashamed

Typical Christian: "I hesitate to speak about Christ because I suspect it will be embarrassing and people won't be interested".

The Apostle Paul: "I am eager to preach the gospel". Let's see why...

An eagerness

Read Romans 1:8-13

> ❓ *What is Paul's relationship with the church in Rome?*
> ❓ *What can he offer them?*
> ❓ *What does he hope to see among them?*

An obligation

Read Romans 1:14-15

Imagine someone gave you a gift to pass on to a mutual friend. The gift is in your possession, but really it belongs to the person you have been tasked with giving it to. You're obliged to pass it on. That's what Paul means when he says "I am a debtor". God has given us the gift of the gospel. But it's not just for us. We have an obligation to pass it on.

A confidence

Read Romans 1:16-17

These verses set the agenda for the letter as a whole. The "righteousness" or justice of God can mean the rightness by which God judges. But in itself that's *not* good news, for it means we're all rightly condemned. But the righteousness of God also describes a gift God gives—the gift of being declared right with God even though we deserve

condemnation. Paul's going to explain how this works in the rest of the letter, but for now he emphasises these two foundational gospel truths:

- anyone can be right with God—it's for both Jews and Gentiles (v 16), and...

- it is by faith alone that we can be right with God (v 17).

🔽 Apply

Paul uses the word "for" three times in these verses and it reveals the logic of his passion to speak of Christ:

- I am eager to preach (v 15).

- I am not ashamed of the gospel (v 16a).

- The gospel is the power of God ("because" in NIV) (v 16b).

- The gospel reveals the righteousness of God (v 17).

> ❓ *How do these verses answer my suspicions that it will be embarrassing if I speak about Jesus and that people won't be interested?*

We grow our passion for evangelism by being convinced that the gospel is God's power in the world and the only way people can be right with him.

> ❓ *How can we grow that conviction?*

Prayerfully reading Romans is a great start!

Bible in a year: 2 Chronicles 10-12 • Luke 6:27-49

Do you believe in atheists?

"What may be known about God is plain," says verse 19. So why are some people atheists? And why do many more live as if God doesn't exist?

God's self-revelation

Read Romans 1:18-20

> ❓ *What is plain and clear (v 19-20)?*
> ❓ *Why do people not believe the truth (v 18)?*

The reason people don't believe in God is not due to a lack of evidence. The problem is people "suppress the truth by their wickedness" (v 18). People discount the evidence because they don't want to be accountable to God or recognise their need for him.

Paul traces this back to the beginning of the human story...

Read Romans 1:21-25

Humanity didn't want to submit to God (by glorifying God) or admit its need (by giving thanks). Ever since the fall we've twisted the evidence to fit the way we want to live. It's not that people are in the dark and therefore reject God. Instead, they reject God and therefore they're in the dark.

Verse 25 says deep in the heart of every person is a double problem:

- We believe lies instead of believing God.

- We treasure created things instead of treasuring God.

We're caught in a vicious circle: we believe lies because we don't want to honour God and we don't want to honour God because we believe lies about him.

God's wrath-revelation

This section begins: "the wrath of God is being revealed" (v 18). Verses 18-25 explain why. Now, Paul describes what this looks like in everyday life.

Read Romans 1:26-32

> ❓ *How is God's wrath being revealed?*
> ❓ *How do you see this is in contemporary society? Think of some concrete examples.*

Three times Paul says "God gave them over..." (v 24, 26, 28). In his grace God restrains many of the effects of sin (by conscience, empathy, family obligations, peer pressure, the rule of law)—otherwise humanity would be overwhelmed by violent anarchy.

But also in his grace God lifts that restraint, so that we get a glimpse of the ugliness of sin. It's a warning of the wrath that's still to be fully revealed (2:5). Remember, too, these sins are not the real problem; they're a sign of the real problem which is our failure to trust and honour God. That's why the transforming power of the gospel must be the only solution—not just moral reform.

⌃ Pray

Pray that God would bring light to the darkened hearts of unbelievers you know.

Bible in a year: 2 Chronicles 13-14 • Luke 7:1-30

Judgment and kindness

The gospel is the good news that we can be right with God through faith in Christ (1:17). But if we must be made right that means something must be wrong.

That's exactly what we see all around us (1:18-32). All is not right with the world. Have another quick look at 1:29-31.

❓ *What do you make of these behaviours?*

Paul anticipates one kind of reaction in 2:1.

Read Romans 2:1

❓ *Who is Paul talking to?*
❓ *What do they make of the revelation of God's wrath in 1:18?*
❓ *What judgment do they make on the behaviours described in 1:29-31?*
❓ *What judgment does the gospel make on such people?*

Paul is talking to apparently moral people who look down their noses at immoral people. They assume the wrath revealed in 1:18-32 is for other people—criminals, scroungers, adulterers, deviants. But Paul says their judgment on other people rebounds on them. Let's see why.

I'm not as bad as others!

Read Romans 2:2-3

People often say, "I'm not as bad as others". As long as there are people they can look down on, they feel ok. There are two problems with this attitude. First, God's judgment "is based on truth" (v 2). God has given us a universal standard in his law. Scoring slightly better than your neighbour carries no weight when the pass mark is 100 percent.

Second, God isn't interested in outward respectability. He looks at "your stubbornness and your unrepentant heart" (v 5, see also v 16).

I enjoy God's kindness!

People today don't want to hear about judgment. They prefer to think of God as kind. And God *is* kind. But we mustn't misinterpret God's kindness.

Read Romans 2:4-5

❓ *What is God doing in the present?*
❓ *What will God do in the future?*
❓ *Why has God delayed his full judgment?*

God is revealing his judgment as we see the impact of sin in our culture (1:18). But this is only a preview of a coming "day of God's wrath" (2:5). God's judgment is backing up like water behind a dam until the day God pours it out on humanity (v 5).

Why the delay? To give people the opportunity to repent before it is too late (v 4).

⌄ Apply

❓ *When do you look down on others?*
❓ *How should the judgment and kindness of God reshape your attitudes?*
❓ *How should these two truths shape how you talk with others this week?*

Is God's judgment fair?

Is it fair for God to judge those who have not heard about him and his law? It's a question that sometimes comes up as we share the gospel with others.

Judged by our works

Read Romans 2:6

We're not saved by works. As Paul makes clear in 1:17, we're saved *only* by faith. But we are *judged* by works. Paul quotes the Old Testament in 2:6 to demonstrate that everyone is repaid according to what they've done.

Read Romans 2:7-11

❓ *What is Paul's argument here?*

Verses 7 and 10 may describe the result of "the obedience that comes from faith" (1:5) or they may describe what would have happened if humanity had honoured God. 2:7 picks up the "glory", "honour" and "immortality" language of 1:21-23. This is the way humanity *should* have responded to God's revelation in creation. If we had done so then we would have received eternal life. But instead we swapped lies for truth and followed evil instead of honouring God (1:23; 2:8). The result is divine wrath and anger (2:9).

Judged by the law

Read Romans 2:12-16

❓ *What is Paul's argument here?*

Paul shows why everyone deserves God's judgment. First, Jews and other religious people deserve judgment because they've not obeyed the law. Hearing the law, knowing the Bible, going to church, and listening to good preaching are not enough. What counts is obeying the law and no one has consistently kept the law. So "all who are under the law will be judged by the law" (v 12). But what about those who don't have the Scriptures?

Judged by our conscience

Read Romans 2:12-16 again

❓ *What is Paul's argument here?*

Paul says God has written his law on our hearts. That's what conscience is—a divinely-given sense of right and wrong. Every time we follow our conscience we show that we have this sense of right and wrong. And if we have a sense of right and wrong then it's reasonable for God to judge us accordingly. No one can plead ignorance in God's court. So "all who sin apart from the law will also perish apart from the law" (v 12).

So no one has a good reason why they should escape God's judgment—at least not until we discover in chapter 3 that God himself has provided a way of escape in Jesus. But before Paul introduces us to God's righteousness, he systematically demolishes all human self-righteousness.

☑ Apply

❓ *How would you respond to the claim that God's judgment is unfair?*

When religion goes wrong

In 2:1-16 Paul addressed those who rely on morality. Now he addresses those who rely on religion.

Read Romans 2:17

These people are not claiming to be perfect, but they think their religion makes them ok. Paul's focus is on religious Jews—those who "rely on the law" as the sign they're right with God (v 17). But the same principles apply to nominal churchgoers.

A failed solution

Read Romans 2:17-24

The Jews were God's interim solution to the problem of humanity's sin (the problem described in 1:18 – 2:16). The nation of Israel was supposed to be a guide for the blind (1:18-20). But it all went horribly wrong. Israel failed to live up to the standards she was meant to embody (v 21-23). The solution became part of the problem.

····· TIME OUT ······························

Read Deuteronomy 4:5-8 and Isaiah 2:1-5

❷ *What would have happened if Israel had kept God's law?*

Israel was meant to be a light to the nations. By obeying the law she was supposed to show that it's good to know God and live under his rule. Then the nations would be drawn to the ways of God. But instead Israel was drawn to the ways of the nations. Instead of displaying God's goodness, she made matters worse by damaging God's reputation (Romans 2:24).

A deeper solution

Read Romans 2:25-29

Imagine I have in my wallet a membership card for an exclusive club. It's a sign that I belong. But suppose my subscription has lapsed or I've been banned for bad behaviour. Then my membership card is meaningless.

Circumcision was the "membership card" of Judaism—the sign that you belonged to God. But without "the obedience that comes from faith" (1:5) it was a meaningless sign.

In 2:28-29 Paul uses the word "Jew" to describe a true member of God's people. And it's not about ethnicity or circumcision. It's about an inner transformation by the Holy Spirit. Paul (echoing Deuteronomy 30:6 and Jeremiah 4:4) calls it a "circumcision of the heart". John 3:3-8 calls it being "born again". The Spirit gives spiritual life to dead hearts.

✓ Apply

❷ *How might these verses apply to nominal churchgoers today?*
❷ *How might they become part of the problem?*
❷ *What's the deeper solution to this problem?*

The King's choir

Psalm 145 is the last "of David" psalm in the Psalter—a psalm in which the king leads us in the praise that is so energetically expressed in the final five psalms.

Think of five reasons to praise God. Then...

Read Psalm 145

> ❓ *Now find five more reasons this psalm gives for praising God.*
> ❓ *Do any of the things David lists here surprise you?*
> ❓ *What kind of praise are we called to in verses 1-2?*

The picture in verses 1-2 is of *unreserved, unbroken* and *unending* praise. How can you and I do that? We can't!

Who can praise like this?

The first person to speak verses 1-2 is the king, leading the people in praise. That is what David is doing here.

> ❓ *Could David's praise be unreserved? Unbroken? Unending? Why / why not?*

The psalms kept calling for this wonderful praise, but no Israelite succeeded in giving it until, centuries later, a boy sang the psalms in the synagogue. And—as he grew up as a child, a youth and a young man—every time he heard the call to praise, there was an answering cry in his believing heart: *Yes! Yes, I will praise.* With complete consistency, with integrity, with perseverance and with perfection, Jesus Christ gave the praise that is pledged at the start of this psalm.

Still today, Jesus the King praises God the Father-King: the King praises the King. Or, to put it more accurately, the divine-human King leads his people in praise of God the Father-King. This is such a relief to us. We are not being asked to take the microphone to lead the praise: no, we are invited to join the choir of Jesus and to join in the praise that he is already leading.

Greatness and goodness

> ❓ *In verses 3-13a, is each verse about God's greatness, his goodness, or both?*
> ❓ *What do verses 13b-20 say about God's faithfulness—to the world and to his people?*

The Lord Jesus makes the Father known as the One who is unfailingly faithful to every living being in the whole created order, but above all as the One who demonstrates his unfailing reliability to all who trust him through Jesus. This is where we come in—not to initiate the praise, for Jesus has done that, and not to lead the praise, for Jesus is doing that, but to join the choir.

✔ Apply

> ❓ *What opportunities do you have to join Jesus' choir this week?*
> ❓ *How could you remind yourself to praise God more often?*
> ❓ *What impact might your praise have on those around you?*

 Bible in a year: 2 Chronicles 21-22 • Luke 9:1-17

Can God be trusted?

Paul is explaining how we can be right with God. But perhaps the problem is not with us, but with God.

Paul anticipates three questions that might arise from what he's said in chapters 1 – 2. He'll return to these questions later but for now he deals with them briefly.

What advantage is there in being Jewish?

Read Romans 3:1-2

Paul has just said the Jews are not right with God just because they have the law (2:17). But having the law is a big advantage because it reveals God and his purposes.

Apply

Paul describes the Scriptures as "the very words of God".

> ❷ *Is this how you view the Bible?*
> ❷ *What difference would it make to how you read it and respond to it, if you did?*

Does God break his promises?

Read Romans 3:3-4

> ❷ *What's the accusation against God?*
> ❷ *How does Paul respond?*

God had promised to bless all nations through the Jews. Did that promise fail when Israel failed to point people to God (2:24)? No, the problem wasn't with God's promise, but with their unfaithfulness.

Paul is going to show how God has kept his promises. Indeed human unfaithfulness will reveal God's faithfulness all the more clearly. But that raises another question…

Is God unfair?

Read Romans 3:5-8

> ❷ *What's the accusation against God?*
> ❷ *How does Paul respond?*

Is it fair to judge sin when God has used that sin to reveal his glory? Yes, because sin is still sin. Paul also follows this argument to its logical conclusion in verse 8: the implication that we should "do evil that good may result" is clearly absurd (see 6:1-2).

Jesus makes things right between us and God. But that means that something must be wrong. 3:1-8 shows the problem is not with God: God is in the right ("righteous"). The problem lies elsewhere—with us.

Apply

> ❷ *How would a someone live if they were not confident in the Bible? How would it be different if they were confident?*
> ❷ *How would someone live if they were not confident God was fair? And if they were confident?*
> ❷ *Look at the evidence of your life. Where would you place yourself between lack of confidence and total confidence in God's words and ways?*

Silenced

The gospel is good news. It's the good news that we can be right with God. But to appreciate the good news of salvation we need to reckon first with the bad news.

The story so far

The good news of being made right with God means at the moment we're in the wrong. We need saving from the wrath of God. In chapter 2 Paul systematically dismantled all our excuses and exceptions.

- We can't point to our moral superiority because our own moral standards condemn us (2:1-4).

- We can't point to our religious knowledge because our knowledge of God's law condemns us (2:13).

- We can't claim ignorance because God's law is written on our hearts (2:14-15).

The defence has put its case, but at each turn its claims have been dismissed. Now Paul brings the prosecution case to a climax.

Condemned...

Read Romans 3:9-18

❷ *How would you summarise Paul's argument in these verses?*

Having the Bible is a big advantage (v 1-2), but only if you follow what it says. Otherwise it's no advantage at all (v 9). In 2:17 Paul anticipated a religious person appealing to the law. "I'm ok because I read my Bible and hear it preached each week." Paul replies, *Ok, let's look at what the Bible says.* He then unleashes a torrent of

Scripture that declares our utter, complete and undeniable guilt. The Bible is called by the defendant's lawyer, but when it takes the stand, all it can do is confirm the prosecution's case. Guilty. Utterly guilty.

... one and all

Read Romans 3:19-20

First, Paul showed that Gentiles (non-Jews) are guilty before God—they're condemned by God's revelation in creation and conscience (1:19-20; 2:15). Now he's shown that Jews are also guilty—they're condemned by the law. Far from making us right with God, the law actually shows us that we're in the wrong (3:20). So now the verdict is passed: "the whole world"—Gentiles and Jews—is condemned.

☑ Apply

❷ *What excuses do you make for your sin?*
❷ *What do you do that you feel gives you a right to God's blessing?*

Don't worry—Paul is about to show how faith in Jesus makes us right with God! But for now the only reasonable response we can make is silence (v 19). We must stop making excuses and we must stop thinking that anything we *do* gives us a right to God's blessing.

Talk to God about what we have read today.

By grace, by Christ, by faith

"There is no one righteous, not even one," says Paul in 3:10. If there is to be any hope it must come from outside of us. It must come from God.

Read Romans 3:21

The law was not the solution to the problem of human sin (v 20). But it did point to the solution: a way of being right with God that God himself would provide.

Read Romans 3:22-25

"Justified" means "made righteous" or "right with God".

> ❷ *Look for the words "by" or "through". How can we be right with God?*

Notice the three elements of God's salvation that Paul draws our attention to here:

- **It is planned by grace (v 24):** Grace is God's undeserved kindness. What we deserve is condemnation (3:19-20); what we're offered is acquittal.

- **It is achieved by Jesus (v 24-25):** We couldn't make ourselves right with God. So God sent Jesus. Jesus redeemed us from the power of sin and paid the penalty that sin requires.

- **It is received by faith (v 22-23, 25):** This righteousness (being right with God) is given, and like any gift it's not earned, but received. We silence all our claims to be righteous (v 19) and instead entrust ourselves to Jesus.

The justification of God
Read Romans 3:25-26

> ❷ *How does forgiveness in the past bring God's righteousness or justice into question?*
> ❷ *How does justifying those with faith in the present bring God's righteousness into question?*
> ❷ *How does the sacrifice of Christ vindicate God's justice?*

God is just and always acts in a just way. So he can't sweep sin under the carpet. And yet God declares those with faith in Jesus to be in the right even though we're clearly in the wrong! How is that right?

God hasn't ignored our sin. Jesus bore its penalty in full at the cross. God can acquit us because he condemned Jesus in our place. So at the cross God justified us, but he also justified himself. God demonstrated that he is in the right when he makes us in the right, even though we're in the wrong, because Jesus paid the penalty of the wrong we have done.

⌃ Pray

No condemnation now I dread;
Jesus, and all in him, is mine!
Alive in him, my living Head,
and clothed in righteousness divine,
bold I approach the eternal throne,
and claim the crown, through Christ my own.
> *From "And can it be" by Charles Wesley*

Don't put others in the dock

Yesterday we saw that we can be right with God by faith in Christ. We're used to applying this to ourselves, but Paul also encourages us to apply it to others.

No one can boast

If we could get right with God through our good works, religious heritage or Bible knowledge then we might have reasons to boast.

Read Romans 3:27-28

> ❓ *What does Paul say about boasting?*
> ❓ *How should justification by faith affect the way we view other Christians?*

The word "law" in verse 27 means "principle". It's a kind of pun. The law of Moses gave people a way of comparing themselves with others and boasting in their superior performance. But the "law" or "principle" of faith sweeps all this away. "By faith" is shorthand for "by faith in what Jesus has done". Our only boast is Jesus (1 Corinthians 1:31).

🔽 Apply

You're a sinner saved by grace. But then so are your fellow Christians. It's easy to look down on Christians who aren't living up to our standards. But what if God did the same towards you? God accepts every Christian through Christ and we need to follow his lead. As we walk free from the courtroom, let's not put others in the dock.

🔼 Pray

Think about someone in your church who annoys or frustrates you. Pray that God would open your eyes so that you see them as he sees them—as righteous in Christ.

No one gets left out

Read Romans 3:29-31

> ❓ *What is the difference between Jews and Gentiles in God's eyes?*
> ❓ *What should Christians think of the law?*

The law of Moses clearly divided Jews and Gentiles (non-Jews). Gentiles could only be saved by becoming Jews. But the faith-principle sweeps this away. Your heritage, upbringing, respectability or knowledge are not what matters. What matters is faith and that means anyone can become right with God. No one need get left out.

If Jesus makes us right with God, rather than keeping the law then can we ditch the law? *No*, says Paul, in verse 31. The law exposes our problem and points us to our solution—Jesus (v 20). This was always its true purpose.

🔼 Pray

Is there someone you think is unlikely to be saved? Since being right with God is by faith, then anyone can be saved. Pray that God would open their eyes so that they put their faith in Jesus.

A bit of accountancy

"This faith idea is all very clever, Paul, but we've been relating to God through the law for centuries. You can't just make up a new way of doing things."

❓ *How does Paul respond to this accusation?*

Read Romans 4:1-3

Abraham was right with God by faith. Paul shows that from the very beginning God's people have *always* been made right with God by faith.

Read Romans 4:4-5

The fact that righteousness is a gift shows that it's not an obligation God owes us because of our works. We have a choice:

* We can relate to God by works and get what we deserve.

* We can relate to God by faith and get what Jesus deserves.

Read Romans 4:6-8

❓ *What does God do (v 6)?*
❓ *What does God not do (v 8)?*

It's time for a bit of spiritual accountancy. Imagine your relationship with God in the form of a bank statement. In the debit column are your sins and in the credit column are your good works. It looks bleak: your righteousness balance is badly in the red. But when you trust in Christ, God wipes out the debt (v 8). But he also credits you with Christ's righteousness (v 6).

⌃ Pray

Think of all the blessings King David enjoyed in his life. The blessing that really matters, says David, is to have your sins forgiven (v 7). Thank God that through Jesus your sins are forgiven.

Read Romans 4:9-12

Was Abraham counted right with God because he was circumcised? *No,* because Abraham wasn't circumcised when he was first counted right with God. Circumcision came later as a sign of what had already happened. So Abraham is the father of:

* those who have faith and are circumcised, and...

* those who have faith and are not circumcised (as Abraham was when he was first counted right with God).

···· TIME OUT ·····

Check for yourself whether Paul is right...

Read Genesis 15:6 and 17:24

❓ *Which came first—righteousness or circumcision?*

⌄ Apply

Auditors scrutinise accounts to check a company is financially healthy. It's easy for us to feel we're being spiritually scrutinised. Maybe you feel under a cloud of spiritual debt—never able to do enough to please God. But we don't need to live like this: God has wiped out your debt and credited righteousness against your name.

Many nations

God has a plan to save people from all nations with the gospel of Jesus, and you can be part of that plan.

"What me? I'm just an ordinary Christian. I'm not cut out for missionary work!"

Read Romans 4:13-17

> ❷ *What was Abraham promised (v 13)?*
> ❷ *How did he receive this promise (v 13)?*
> ❷ *What happens if we depend on keeping the law (v 14-15)?*
> ❷ *How can we have confidence in God's promise (v 16-17)?*

God's plan to save people from all nations started when God promised to bless all nations through Abraham. That plan first came by faith and it's continued to be by faith. Faith is not a task we have to accomplish. "By faith" is shorthand for "by faith in God's power to do what he has promised'" (v 21). The plan to save people from all nations rests on God's ability to give life to the dead (v 17). Whenever the plan has seemed to hit a dead end, God has turned the situation around.

Case study #1: Isaac

Read Romans 4:18-22

> ❷ *What was the threat to God's plan to save people from all nations through Abraham?*
> ❷ *How did God overcome that threat?*

Abraham's body was "as good as dead" (v 19). But God brought life from death when Sarah conceived their son, Isaac.

Case study #2: Jesus

Read Romans 4:23-24

> ❷ *What was the threat to God's plan to save people from all nations?*
> ❷ *How did God overcome that threat?*

Jesus was dead and it looked like the plan was in ruins. But God raised Jesus from the dead—the ultimate sign of God's power to deliver his promise.

Case study #3: Us

Read Romans 4:25

We were dead in our sins. But Jesus took our sins on himself when he died. Now his resurrection is his vindication (a declaration that he's in the right) and therefore also our vindication (a declaration that we're in the right).

⌄ Apply

> ❷ *How do these verses give us confidence that we can be right with God through Jesus?*
> ❷ *How do these verses give us confidence in God's ability to use ordinary people like us to save people from all nations?*

⌃ Pray

How does God's plan depend on his power to bring life from death? Re-read verse 20, then join Abraham in giving glory to God.

Praise matters

Psalm 148 is a wonderful and beautiful psalm. But it is not a comfortable psalm. And it can never be a psalm simply about creation.

Read Psalm 148

❷ *Who and what are told to praise God in verses 1-4? Do any of these surprise you?*

❷ *Why are they to praise God (v 5-6)?*

The "angels" in their "heavenly hosts" (v 2) are supernatural spirits, lower than God (for they are not divine) and yet greater than humans. They can decide whether or not to praise, and it seems that some rebelled (Jude 6). It seems that the devil and his evil spirits are fallen angels. So this is not a superfluous cry: praise him, *all* his angels!

❷ *How do you think inanimate objects like the sun, moon and stars can give praise (Psalm 148:3)?*

Psalm 148: 5-6 help us to understand. First, these objects were *created*. Second, God *established* them and "issued a decree that will never pass away" (v 6). The heavenly bodies praise God by being what they are and doing what they do. In their regularity, they speak of his faithfulness; in their variety, of his creativity; in their wonder, of his beauty. And we too, as created beings, praise God by living in line with the order and purpose for which he has created us.

⌄ Apply

This reminds us never to worship the sun, moon, stars, spirits, angels or saints (and not to look at horoscopes). And it reminds us to worship the One who made all those things, and who set each in its place.

Verses 7-10 list more created things that praise God by doing his bidding (v 8).

❷ *Is that also true of those in verses 11-12?*

Everything else praises God, but human beings do not, and will not, heed this call to praise. For, as Paul so graphically puts it in Romans 1:21-32, we have exchanged the proper worship of the Creator for a twisted worship of created things. This is why we need the surprise of the final verse.

Read Psalm 148:13-14 again

"Horn" in biblical imagery symbolises strength and power, wielded by a ruler. It is used often in the Old Testament about God's anointed King, the Messiah who is to come. Now Jesus—this anointed "horn", this strong Messiah—is recreating the human race so that it exhibits fully the image of God.

This can never be a psalm simply about creation. It must necessarily be about redemption also. The most urgent need of the created order is not creation care; it is the gospel of Jesus Christ the anointed King. He is the strong "horn", who will raise up a people close to God's heart—a new, redeemed humanity who will take their proper place in the created order, living a life of obedient praise to their Creator.

❷ *How will you give God the praise he so richly deserves, not just with your words but also your actions?*

Therefore, since…

"Therefore, since…" begins verse 1. These words introduce the results of being right with God.

Paul has shown how we can be right with God through faith in Jesus. But so what? What difference does this make?

Read Romans 5:1-2

> ❓ *What are the consequences of being justified or right with God?*

Our rebellion against God was a declaration of war. But Jesus has brought peace. And that also means access to God and his grace. And there is more to come: one day we will enjoy the glory of God.

··· **TIME OUT** ··

Read Colossians 1:19-22

> ❓ *How do these verses describe our past?*
> ❓ *How do they describe our present status? What has made the difference?*

Read Romans 5:2-4

The word "boast" in verse 2 is the same word as "glory" in verse 3.

> ❓ *What is our boast or glory in verse 2? Why?*
> ❓ *What is our boast or glory in verse 3? Why?*

It's easy to see why we might boast in the hope of glory. But why should we boast in suffering? Because in God's hands suffering can increase our hope. Hope is like a muscle—it grows strong when it's exercised. And suffering is like a spiritual exercise regime. Suffering forces us to look ahead to the glory. If we just look at our circumstances then we might give up. But if we look ahead then we can persevere. So suffering produces perseverance. Do that enough times and it becomes a habit; repeat a habit enough times and it becomes your character.

✔ Apply

> ❓ *Can you think of people you know whose character and hope have grown as they've persevered through suffering?*
> ❓ *What do you find appealing about them?*

No shame

Read Romans 5:5

Imagine standing before God on the day of judgment. You're about to hear God's verdict on your life. All the evidence points to a guilty verdict. But you hope to hear the words "not guilty" because you've put your faith in Jesus. This hope, says verse 5, is not a vague sense of optimism. We will not walk from God's courtroom in shame. How can we be so sure? Because God has already given us the Holy Spirit. The Spirit is the sign that we've received God's life and God's love (as we'll see when we reach chapter 8).

✖ Pray

Praise God for the benefits of being right with him through faith in Jesus.

God's love demonstration

On the final day we'll hear the words, "Not guilty". But what if we mess up badly between now and then?

Perhaps you trust God to be faithful to you. But you're not so sure about yourself. Is it possible that you can wreck your salvation?

Read Romans 5:6-11

- ❓ *What do these verses say took place in the past?*
- ❓ *What is true in the present?*
- ❓ *What will happen in the future?*

Undeserved love

Read Romans 5:6-8 again

Christ died for us while we were still weak and "while we were still sinners". That's what marks out God's love as special. Being sacrificial for worthy people is one thing, but Christ was sacrificial for unworthy people.

How do you know God loves you? It's wonderful when we're moved by God's love—perhaps during a great sermon or a time of worship. But if this is what your confidence rests on then it will only ever be as good as your last experience. And what if your last experience was a cancer diagnosis or a broken heart?

The good news is that the great demonstration of God's love is the cross. When our hearts are thrown into turmoil by our circumstances, we can *always* look to the cross and be confident in God's love for us.

Unending love

Read Romans 5:9-11 again

- ❓ *What did God do in the past (v 10-11)?*
- ❓ *What has happened in the present (v 9)?*
- ❓ *What will happen in the future (v 9, 11)?*

Paul's logic is simple: since God reconciled us to himself in the past when we were his enemies, we can be even more confident that he'll save us in the future now that we're his friends. You may mess up or fall into sin. But remember that's what you were like when God first loved you!

✓ Apply

Using these verses, how would you encourage or help a fellow Christian who comes to you filled with doubts about God, the gospel or his own salvation?

⌃ Pray

Praise God for the past, present and future of your salvation.

Death's days numbered

100 percent of us will die. No one escapes death for its reign is universal. Or at least it that was the case before Christ …

❓ *Why does our culture fear death?*

How sin entered
Read Romans 5:12

❓ *What were the consequences of Adam's sin (v 12)?*

Death is an outrageous intrusion into God's good world. It came as a result of Adam's sin. God appointed Adam as the head or representative of humanity. When a prime minister or president declares war, everyone in the country is at war—even though they themselves didn't make the decision. When Adam declared war on God, everyone in Adam became at war with God.

Read Romans 5:13-14 and 20

God's law does not make us sinners. But it does turn our rebellion into "transgressions"—specific acts of law breaking (4:15; 5:20). In this way the law exposes our hatred of God by giving it visible form.

The same but different
Read Romans 5:15-19

❓ *What are the similarities between Adam and Christ?*
❓ *What are the differences between Adam and Christ?*
❓ *What did Adam do and what were the consequences?*
❓ *What did Jesus do and what were the consequences?*

Verse 14 describes Adam as "a pattern of the one to come". Adam is the representative of the old humanity and Jesus is the representative of a new humanity—those who are in him by faith.

Is it fair for God to deal with us on the basis of someone else's actions? It is God's way and he is *always* fair. But also ask yourself this: would you rather God dealt with you on the basis of your actions or Christ's?

Verse 15 says: "But the gift is not like the trespass". Christ's act and its results are the exact opposite of Adam's act and its results. What flows from Adam and Christ is shown below:

Adam: disobedience ➜ condemnation ➜ death

Christ: obedience ➜ justification ➜ life

⌃ Pray
Read Romans 5:20-21

- Death reigns in our world (v 14, 17, 21).

- Christ brings a new reign of life (v 17, 18, 21).

- Death is an outrageous intrusion in the world, but its days are numbered.

Praise God for these truths.

Regime change

Resisting temptation is tough. So why bother when God forgives sin?

Read Romans 6:1

> ❷ *What's the question that Paul is addressing?*

TIME OUT

Read Romans 3:22-24; 4:7; 5:20

> ❷ *Why does Paul anticipate people asking this question in 6:1?*

Read Romans 6:2-7

> ❷ *What's Paul's response to the suggestion that it's ok to continue to sin?*

Is sin ok? "By no means!" says Paul. Becoming a Christian is not just a change of worldview or allegiance. It's a death and a resurrection experience.

> ❷ *Go through verses 2-7 and in each verse see how Paul says or implies that we have died to sin.*
> ❷ *What does it mean to have died to sin?*

Some say it describes a state Christians can reach in which sin no longer influences them. But this doesn't fit the link with Christ's death to sin, since he was never under its influence (v 10). Nor does it fit Paul's need to call us to stop sinning (v 11-13).

Others say it means Christians have died to the *penalty* of sin. This is part of it. But Paul goes further.

It's important to see the link between chapters 5 and 6. Our "old self" in 6:6 is our "old humanity"—humanity in Adam (the same word is used of "all people" or "all men" in 5:12). Christians used to be part of this old humanity, but we're now part of a new humanity in Christ. How do we make this move? In Christ and through baptism (6:3-4). In Christ's death and resurrection we died to the old humanity and were raised to a new life. We have been freed from the reign or authority of sin—which is exactly what Paul says in 5:21.

We're no longer under the *authority* of sin. But we're not yet free from the *influence* of sin. (That may be what Paul means by "the body ruled by sin" in 6:6.) Sin still affects our thinking, desires, instincts, habits and fears (both individually and socially).

We still struggle with the influence of sin, even though it holds no power over us.

☑ Apply

The main application is coming in verses 11-14. But for now consider this: Christians always have a choice *not to sin*. Sometimes giving in to temptation can feel inevitable. It's not! Not if you're a Christian. Sin is no longer your master.

Think yourself holy

Christians have moved from the old humanity under the reign of death and sin into a new humanity under the reign of life and grace.

It's as if we've switched nationality. But we've not switched nationality by passing a citizenship test—we badly failed God's citizenship test (3:23). Something much more radical has happened. We've died as members of the old regime of sin and we've been raised as members of the new regime of grace.

"But surely I would have remembered dying," you might be thinking! We died with Christ (6:3-4). His death was our death and his life is our life.

No turning back
Read Romans 6:8-10

> ❓ *What's the relationship between Christ and death and sin?*
> ❓ *What's the relationship of those in Christ to death and sin?*

Jesus placed himself under the authority of sin in the sense that he submitted to the penalty required for sin by the law: death. But now the price is paid. So sin has no further claim on Christ—nor on those in Christ. And death has no authority over Christ—nor on those in Christ. There's no route back into slavery!

⌄ Apply

> ❓ *Where are you particularly tempted to turn back to futile, sinful ways?*

Forward to freedom
Read Romans 6:11-14

> ❓ *What are we to do now that we're free from the authority of sin?*

"Consider" or "count" yourself dead to sin is not an act of make-believe. The way we think about ourselves has got to catch up with the reality of what has taken place in Christ (v 11). We still feel the influence of sin (we still have "passions" or "evil desires"), but we're not under its "reign" or authority (v 12). Our thinking and behaviour is to match our new identity as members of the new humanity under the reign of grace (v 14).

⌃ Pray
Read Romans 6:13 again

> ❓ *Think about whether each part of your body is used for wickedness or righteousness:*
> * *Your ears (what you listen to)*
> * *Your eyes (what you watch)*
> * *Your mouth (what you say)*
> * *Your stomach (what you eat)*
> * *Your hands (what you do)*
> * *Your feet (where you go)*
> * *Your brain (what you think about)*

Now offer each part to the service of God.

A new master

What are the controlling influences on your life? If someone looked closely at your life, where would they conclude that your allegiance lay?

Influences

Read Romans 6:15

❓ *Why do you think this question is repeated?*

Romans 6:15-23 offers the same response to the same question as 6:1-14. But Paul changes the imagery. Instead of talking about regime change, he talks about having a new master.

Read Romans 6:16-19

❓ *What is Paul's argument in these verses?*

In practice people are slaves to whoever they obey (v 16). If you obey sin then you live as if you're a slave to sin. But Christians are not slaves to sin any more (v 17-18). Offering ourselves to sin is massively inconsistent with our new status in Christ. Instead we're to live as slaves to righteousness which means obeying what righteousness requires (v 19).

Imagine a slave who has been set free from a cruel master. One day she meets her old master. Without thinking, she cowers in fear. When the old master barks a command she instinctively moves to obey. The old master still has real *influence* over her. But he no longer has *authority* over her. She can and should tell herself, "I don't have to do what he says and I don't have to fear his rebuke".

That is what Christians are called to say: "Sin has no authority over me. I don't have to do what sin says and I don't have to fear its rebuke."

Consequences

Read Romans 6:20-23

❓ *Where does slavery to sin lead?*
❓ *Where does slavery to God lead?*

Notice that in verse 22 holiness is a benefit (or fruit), not a requirement. It's not the case that we have to earn eternal life by being holy. Both holiness and life are benefits of Christ's liberating work. That's why in verse 23 sin pays a wage (death) but God gives a gift (life).

···· TIME OUT ··

Read Exodus 4:23

The word translated "worship" or "serve" is used to describe Israel's slavery under Pharaoh. In the exodus God's people moved from slavery to Pharaoh through the waters of the Red Sea to serving God (which is actually true freedom). In Romans 6 Paul tells the story of our exodus in Christ from slavery to sin through the waters of baptism to serving God.

Pray

Praise God for these truths.

Where true strength lies

We're taking a rest from our Sunday series in the Psalms to work our way through Proverbs. In hard times we look to strong leaders, close family and solid financial reserves. But where does true strength really come from?

How to build a house

Read Proverbs 24:1-4

- ❓ *Why is it so tempting to "envy the wicked" (v 1)?*
- ❓ *What do we think we will get from spending time in their company?*
- ❓ *Who do you think "the wicked" are here against whom the writer is warning us?*
- ❓ *Why is it such a big mistake to envy them and to seek their fellowship (v 2-4)?*
- ❓ *What is it that will truly deliver what we are after?*

Wisdom is not just *knowing* things; it is *seeing* the world as God sees it, understanding how life really works with God as King. For us in the gospel age, it is understanding what our role is and not being distracted from it. Many of those who the world admires for their money-making ability, are, deep down, ruthless individuals who are quite prepared to ride roughshod over others in pursuit of their plans. They may not be murderers, but they use strong-arm tactics to get what they want. Genuine, God-aware wisdom, however, is the only thing that will truly build a house worth living in. A career that honours God; a family that serves the Lord; a church that is reaching out with the gospel; a Christian work that is faithful to the Bible—all these "houses" (v 3) are filled with beautiful treasures (v 4). Their walls may be bare of oil paintings and *objets d'art*, but the treasures of love and refined faith will make this a house worth living in.

✔ Apply

- ❓ *In what ways do you find yourself most likely to envy the wicked?*
- ❓ *How can you remind yourself at those moments of what is truly valuable?*

Real power

Read Proverbs 24:5-7

- ❓ *Where does real power lie?*
- ❓ *How can we make sure we stay wise and avoid foolishness?*

The particular thing in view here is warfare, but the principle is the same in all of life—which is spiritual warfare. Those with worldly power and wealth may make us feel ignorant, irrelevant or, increasingly, evil. But sticking to God's way of living and viewing ourselves and everyone else through the lens of the Gospel message is the route to genuine power. And we need the encouragement, advice and input from "many advisors"—the genuine fellowship of believers—in order to sustain us in living that way, thinking that way. As we approach the Christmas season, let's remember that God's powerful plan of salvation began with a helpless baby in a manger.

◣ Pray

Thank God for your brothers and sisters in Christ. Pray that you would be able to encourage them in godly living and thinking today.

CHRISTMAS: True story

Strange visitations by angelic beings and then a mysterious birth to a virgin? God becoming man! Stories like this were common in the ancient world, but this is different…

Roving researcher

Read Luke 1:1-4

❓ *What does Luke want his first readers to get from his Gospel (v 4)?*

❓ *What does he say in these verses that would give them (and us) this confidence?*

❓ *What methods did Luke use to compile his account?*

Luke claims to have written a work of investigative journalism. He has carefully searched through:

- **Written reports.** It seems they were not short of documents in the ancient world that recorded the teaching and other details of Jesus' life and death. He says that there were "many" (v 1). But Luke doesn't just take these as "gospel"…

- **Eyewitnesses.** He talks to those who were actually there. His gospel narrative isn't cobbled together from things that happened to "a friend of a friend". *No.* Luke takes the trouble to check out, and presumably correct and supplement the earlier written documents by interviewing people who were actually there.

- **Careful investigation.** Luke, who is elsewhere described as a physician (Colossians 4:14), is clearly a man of serious learning, with an enquiring mind. He pieces together the various bits of evidence and writes them up as an "orderly account". This means that it is grouped in an organised way, not necessarily written in the order that it happened.

TIME OUT

Theophilus (a Greek name meaning "lover of God") may have been a wealthy patron who Luke sent his Gospel to. Or it could be that this is a kind of code word for God's people, i.e. that it was written for the early church—those who love God.

Truth teller

Read Luke 1:1 again

But Luke says he's doing more than just recording events—he's writing about the things that have been "fulfilled" (NIV) or "accomplished" (ESV) among them. He reminds us that these events of Jesus' birth, life, death and resurrection are part of something much bigger. They are part of the story of God's dealing with mankind from the very beginning, and how the fact of Jesus coming into the world changes everything, for everyone, for all time.

⌃ Pray

We all sometimes feel that the Bible is a bit "unreal". Pray that, as you read Luke's account of Jesus' birth, you will become more convinced of its historical truth. And pray that this Christmastime, you would have opportunities to tell others about the reality of Jesus and what he accomplished for us.

Silent witness

Like no other Gospel writer, Luke tells us the remarkable events leading up to Jesus'
birth, weaving into his account the birth of Jesus' forerunner, John the Baptist.

After his introduction, where he is at pains to underline that he is writing history, Luke introduces us to John's parents.

Godly but childless
Read Luke 1:5-10

❓ *What kind of people were Zechariah and Elizabeth?*

❓ *How would their childlessness have been viewed by their culture (see v 25)?*

❓ *How might they have viewed it themselves, do you think?*

To be childless was a sure sign, so people imagined, of God's rejection. But does that fit with verse 6? It's not the message of verse 9 either; it was a great once-in-a-lifetime privilege to burn incense, and guess who controlled the lot which chose Zechariah for this task!

Your prayer is heard
Read Luke 1:11-13

While the crowds were waiting outside, Zechariah was having the shock of his life. And the angel's message was as startling as his appearance. A baby! But they'd long given up hope... it was impossible... they were old people... and yet God had heard those heartfelt prayers after all. And what an answer he was about to give them!

❓ *What does that teach us about all those prayers you thought God hadn't noticed?*

It's a great mistake to assume that God is angry or absent when we go through deep trouble. God brought Elizabeth's richest blessing through her most painful trial.

Powerful promise
Read Luke 1:14-25

❓ *What remarkable promises does the angel give about the child?*

❓ *How should Zechariah have responded to this promise?*

❓ *What do we learn about God's promises by the way the story plays out?*

The child would bring tremendous joy (v 14)—not just to the astonished and delighted parents, but to many others too. He would also be great in God's eyes (v 15), and filled with God's Spirit. Devout and devoted parents all want their children to exceed their own devotion to God. Elizabeth and Zechariah's prayers would be powerfully answered, as their son would be God's instrument for bringing revival to Israel.

Pray

God is not reluctant to answer prayer. It's just that he has far greater plans in mind than we do. Prayer is not trying to coax a reluctant God to give us what we want, but yielding ourselves to the will of God, who has far bigger ambitions for us than we can imagine.

Big baby

Gabriel's second task was to bear news far more staggering and wonderful than the first message. And to whom would the angel be sent? An ordinary young woman.

Highly favoured
Read Luke 1:26-30

> ❓ *The appearance of an angel is troubling, but what is Mary disturbed by (v 29)?*

What a proof that God loves the humble! Mary had nothing going for her, humanly speaking. She lived in the despised town of Nazareth and was engaged to a lowly carpenter. We can readily understand Mary being startled by the angel suddenly appearing. But it's Gabriel's words that bother her most; "troubled" that she, of all women, could be counted favoured by God! What beautiful humility shines from Mary's whole response.

> ❓ *Had she forgotten the truth of Isaiah 57:15?*

Mind-blowing
Read Luke 1:31-34

> ❓ *Weigh the words of Gabriel's promises to Mary. What does each phrase mean?*
> ❓ *What does her response tell us about her attitude and character?*

If Mary was amazed that she had been favoured by God, imagine how her mind would be reeling when the angel explained just what that would mean... Mary surely did not grasp the full significance of what was being said. She did not have time to stop and think through each phrase to appreciate its wonder. But we can take it more slowly; this glorious King of kings growing from a human embryo to a full-grown baby in the womb of an ordinary girl.

Mary believed that it would happen as the angel had said, but how? Was she to marry Joseph first? The angel's reply would certainly be a severe test of her faith...

Heavenly conception
Read Luke 1:35-38

> ❓ *Weigh the words of Gabriel's promises to Mary. What does each phrase mean?*
> ❓ *What does her response tell us about her attitude and character?*

Consider the wonder of conception. The intricate complexity of a fully functioning human springing from two tiny cells—male and female. But the origin of Mary's child would be totally different, conceived by God's Holy Spirit. He would have no other biological father than God—an awesome thought for Mary to come to terms with.

Mary must face the stigma of being pregnant, but not married. Probably her family would reject her, and surely Joseph would now despise her. But Mary does not seem to be worried; there is a beautiful serenity about her reply. No objections about the difficulties, no further questions about how all these things could happen. Just a desire to be the Lord's servant, just a quiet submission to her Lord's will.

Good news shared

Mary was quick to follow up the news brought by the angel; she couldn't wait to share the good news with Elizabeth.

Spirit-filled

Read Luke 1:39-45

Whether or not Mary spilled the beans in her greeting, it was not she who convinced Elizabeth of the truth...

> ❓ *What did?*
> ❓ *What else did the Spirit reveal to her?*
> ❓ *How did this Spirit-filled woman encourage her cousin?*

When believers are filled with God's Holy Spirit, they begin to overflow. Elizabeth could not help crying out with joy and worship. But notice what form this takes: she is filled with the sense of her own unworthiness, and with wonder that God should bring such blessing to her.

Blessing and honour

Read Luke 1:46-56

> ❓ *What were the blessings Mary was overwhelmed with?*
> ❓ *What earth-shattering impact does she see her child would have on the world?*
> ❓ *What words does she use to describe the character of God in this song?*
> ❓ *Why did these truths particularly thrill Mary, do you think?*
> ❓ *How has God acted in respect of his promises?*
> ❓ *In verses 50-54, how has he acted towards "those who fear him" (those who are needy)? And towards the proud?*

Verse 47 could indicate that Mary was already looking to her baby as the one who would save her from her sins, though her understanding would have been rather hazy.

She knew that God is mighty... holy... merciful. These were not just words in Mary's mind, as they can be in our prayers. Expressions of God's character are embedded in the prayers you find in the Bible. They are the source of so much praise, and the grounds for our motivation to pray. If you want to praise God, then spend time considering who he is.

It's hard to separate who he is from what he does—for God's character is always expressed in how he acts.

▲ Pray

> ❓ *Has God done 'great things' for you? What exactly?*
> ❓ *Has he brought about wonderful changes in your life? Has he shown Jesus to be your Saviour?*

If so, then verse 47 is yours as well. Mary spills out reasons to praise God because her heart is bursting with love for God's amazing grace.

It's a great moment for you to do the same...

Birthday surprise

As today, the birth of a child was a time of tremendous joy and interest, not just for the family but for friends and neighbours too.

And it is easy to imagine the stir caused by a couple the age of Elizabeth and Zechariah having a child. Evidently the family wanted a say in choosing the name too...

His name is John

Read Luke 1:57-63

Zechariah was such an appropriate name (meaning "The Lord has remembered"); it was usual to take a family name and the family would be offended otherwise. But there was no room for manoeuvre; Elizabeth and Zechariah were clear—"His name is John". They were not being obstinate; God had made it clear to them in verse 13.

But why John? Surely the forerunner of Jesus was called John for a special reason. John means "The Lord is gracious".

> ❓ *Why is this name especially appropriate? Think about who John was to be.*

What kind of child?

Read Luke 1:64-66

> ❓ *How did the people react?*
> ❓ *What things were making them think?*

The people had been astonished at the parents' choice—and their boldness. But now they could clearly see that God was at work and had a great purpose for the child.

⌄ Apply

If God's word is clear, then we mustn't listen to the persuasive arguments of others who follow what the culture deems to be acceptable!

"They'll be offended"
"We've always done it this way"
"It will cause embarrassment"

Be one of the few who stands up, clearly but graciously, for what God's word says.

> ❓ *What might this need to look like for you specifically in the run-up to Christmas this year?*

⌃ Pray

We do well to notice events showing that hint that God is at work; to react with awe, to wonder, to tell to others what God is doing.

Plead with God that once again he will do things in our lives, in our churches and in our land which will make people really sit up and take notice—so they have to admit: "Surely God is with you; and there is no other".

Prophetic poem

Zechariah made good use of the voice God had given back to him. You can imagine how thankful he was for the gift of his son, John; but John only gets two verses!

Zechariah's best praise is for another child...

Praise him for salvation
Read Luke 1:67-75

> ❷ *What were God's great purposes in visiting the earth with Jesus, the "horn of salvation"? List the things that Jesus would accomplish.*

The language might reflect Zechariah's rather "Israel-based" understanding of the Messiah. But the Holy Spirit inspired him to say rather more than he realised...

⌃ Pray

God's work in salvation through Jesus is the theme of Zechariah's praise—is it ours? Use the headings below to shape your praises as you reflect on the indescribable gift of God's Son.

- He redeems his people (v 68, 69).
- He saves us from our enemies (v 71).
- He keeps his promises (v 72, 73).
- He frees his people to serve him (v 74-75).

Can you thank God for Jesus from the bottom of your heart, knowing that you are one of his people for whom he has such great purposes? If not, then don't be satisfied until you can.

Two verses for his son
Read Luke 1:76-77

> ❷ *What will be the life's work of Zechariah's son?*

Even at this joyful moment for Dad, Zechariah is doing what his son would do—pointing to Jesus! Even the verses about John speak of him preparing the way for Jesus.

John was the prophet who would prepare the way for the Saviour, stirring up the people to be ready for him.

Then back to Jesus
Read Luke 1:78-79

Zechariah is overwhelmed again by God's amazing mercy in sending Jesus.

> ❷ *How is the picture of the rising sun such a beautiful and appropriate picture of the coming of Jesus into the lives of sinners?*

⌄ Apply

Take each phrase in verses 78-79, thinking about how God has made each of these promises real to you through Jesus.

Rescue the weak

As we approach Christmas, it's worth reflecting that those who have been rescued by Christ are also called to be rescuers in turn...

Responsible rescue
Read Proverbs 24:8-12

Verse 10 reminds us that we are frail.

- ❓ *Why is it important to know that as we read verses 11-12?*
- ❓ *Who do you think is in mind in verse 11?*
- ❓ *How does verse 12 address how we avoid thinking about this subject? Does it disturb you?*

These are sobering verses for us. No doubt there are moments when people are in physical danger from which we should seek to rescue them. But more likely in view are those who head down a path of foolishness and threaten to harm themselves and others. For ourselves, we cannot avoid how these verses speak to our attitude towards evangelism. Gospel-sharing is not just a "bolt-on module" to the Christian life—it is at the very heart of why God has chosen us. We are to rescue those who are stumbling down the broad road that leads to destruction. Verse 12 warns us that we can't brush off our responsibility to be evangelists.

···· TIME OUT ····

Read Galatians 6:1-5 and Romans 10:14-17

- ❓ *What encouragement do you find in these passages for your practical and spiritual care of other Christians?*
- ❓ *How do they challenge you in your desire to reach out to others?*

The honey test
Read Proverbs 24:13-14

- ❓ *A father gives his son a practical lesson in valuing wisdom. Picture the scene in your imagination.*

Eat a spoonful of honey, urges the father. We can imagine him saying, "See how wonderful it tastes! Close your eyes and think about the rich sweetness in your mouth, and enjoy the subtle flavours. Just think about the joyful feeling you have as you focus on that experience, and try to capture the feeling. Know, my child, that God's wisdom is just like that. But unlike the honey, which is now just a taste on the lips and will soon be a memory, God's words will lead you to solid joys, lasting treasures and, ultimately, everlasting life."

⌄ Apply

Eat a spoonful of honey and work through the experience and advice of these verses in your own mind. Now ask yourself:

- ❓ *Do you really believe that God's words and wisdom are "honey for the soul"?*
- ❓ *Does your enthusiasm for hearing God's word taught and for reading it day by day show that this is what you really believe?*

Turn your thoughts into prayer.

Christ in Christmas

Some of us seek to remove from our celebrations the excesses of eating, drinking and materialism that characterise a pagan Christmas…

… but even having done so, we are still left far removed from the stark reality of the first Christmas.

The first Christmas

Read Luke 2:1-7

- *What are you most looking forward to on Christmas Day this coming Friday?*
- *What do you notice about the way this story is told?*

Without ceremony, and in complete obscurity, the Son of God enters the world—the place of his birth determined by the decree of a distant emperor, who proclaimed himself God. And yet, unknown, the great Augustus was doing the bidding of the one true God as Jesus is born in Bethlehem, just as the Scriptures foretold.

Apply

It is all too easy to leave Christ out of Christmas…

- *Beyond the traditions and family fun, how should these truths shape how we think about Christmas?*
- *What attitudes and behaviour do you need to pray to avoid?*
- *What practical measures can you take to rejoice in Jesus' birth in a fitting way this Christmas? Write your ideas in the space to the right.*

Look again at verse 7. Think of that love. Think of that poverty. And think of the incalculable riches which that poverty bought for you: "For you know the grace of our Lord Jesus Christ, that though he was rich, yet for your sakes he became poor, so that you through his poverty might become rich" (2 Corinthians 8:9).

The manger was just the beginning of his poverty. A life of loneliness and grief, ending in a death of unutterable sorrow and desolation. That is the true measure of his love.

Pray

Enjoy your Christmas! But pray that you won't let the laughter and fun drown out this message of Jesus' love. Don't let your heart be so crowded out with other things that, like the inn, there is no room for him.

First responders

Mary sang that in Jesus, God would "fill the hungry with good things". We see that starkly illustrated as the message of his birth goes out to a bunch of poor nobodies.

Isaiah's prophecy about Jesus says, "The Spirit of the Sovereign LORD is on me, because the LORD has anointed me to preach good news to the poor. He has sent me to bind up the broken-hearted..." (Isaiah 61:1).

Not first to kings, politicians, the wealthy and privileged, nor even to priests and the religious elite. But to poor, despised, ordinary shepherds.

To the poor
Read Luke 2:8-12

> ❷ *What is the shocking difference between the message (v 11) and the sign (v 12)?*
> ❷ *What three objections to Christianity are countered in verse 10?*

It is good news, not bad; life in Christ is joyful, not miserable; and the message is for *all* people—not just the religious-minded. What a great message this is!

☑ Apply

There are many poor, despised, lonely, sad, unloved people on Christmas day. Christmas seems especially bleak to them; perhaps it does to you? It is people like this that Jesus came to save from sin. Pray that the good news of Jesus, the Saviour, will flood such hearts with intense joy, transforming their lives with Christ's love. And why not knock on doors down your street to invite people who may be isolated to join you?

Praise!

Christmas is not only a time for great joy but for great praise too.

Read Luke 2:13-14

> ❷ *What precisely do the angels praise God for?*

It is understandable that we get tired of singing carols by this stage of the Christmas season, but have you begun yet to lift your voice in heartfelt praise to God for his wonderful gift to you? The shepherds listen in wonder to this dazzling display of heaven's praise for God's work of reconciliation.

☑ Apply

Is there any practical way you can show the love of Christ to sad and lonely people this Christmas? After the year we have had there may be many more who are alone, bereaved, or struggling with isolation.

It's easy as well, to just mechanically "join in" with Christmas carols on autopilot. Determine that you will pause for a moment to tune your heart to praise God before you open your mouth to sing.

"Thank yous" are not always sincere at Christmas. Can you be sincere now as you say your "thank you" for his greatest gift: genuine peace for those who receive the righteousness of Christ?

Finding Christ

It is one thing to hear the good news and believe it to be true. It is quite another to go to Jesus and to know him for yourself.

Short search

Read Luke 2:15-16

Those who seek will find Jesus just as God has promised. But those who find will also have their lives changed by a living encounter with Jesus. The shepherds would go back to their sheep, but they had been transformed by their experience.

Shared message

Read Luke 2:17-19

❷ *What do they immediately do next?*
❷ *Precisely what was the message they passed on (v 17, see v 10-11)?*
❷ *Why is this precision in their message important, do you think?*
❷ *What kind of things do you think Mary was "pondering in her heart"?*

Seeing the child just as they had been told was enough to convince them. Now the shepherds could be sure that this was the Messiah, the Saviour, as the angel had said. But they could not keep the fantastic news to themselves; at the risk of being ridiculed for spinning such a yarn, they broadcast the truth about Jesus.

Witnessing is far from easy. But often it is how we live which makes the real impact. Surely we will not want to keep such life-giving news to ourselves! You may have only been a Christian for a short while. Your understanding of the Bible may be shaky. But

hasn't God done certain things in your life that you are sure of? Hasn't he convinced you of a few life-changing truths? Tell others what God has done for you, even if you can go no further.

Praising God

Read Luke 2:20

❷ *What is the difference, do you think, between glorifying and praising God?*

They rushed to see the truth for themselves. They returned with praise at the wonder of that truth. It's a simple enough chain of events. They heard. They saw. They told. They worshipped.

❷ *Which of these elements of experiencing Christ is most lacking in your Christian life today?*

🔼 Pray

Pray for courage to run the risk of looking stupid as you tell others about what you have heard and seen. Isn't it better to look and feel a little foolish than for others not to realise that Jesus is both Saviour and Lord?

Pray that God would use your faltering testimony to have a similar effect to the shepherds' words. Some who heard were amazed. But at least one who heard remembered all these things, turning them over in her mind.

The law of the Lord

As Jews, Jesus and his parents kept the requirements of the Old Testament law. As he said later, Jesus had not come to destroy the law but to fulfil it perfectly.

Keeping it
Read Luke 2:21-24

❓ *Which two rituals did Jesus go through in obedience to the law?*

❓ *What spiritual significance do these rites have for us today?*

❓ *How will Jesus fulfil both in his life, death and resurrection?*

❓ *What does the name "Jesus' mean?*

Not only did Jesus keep God's law to the letter, but he also fulfilled the spiritual meaning of God's requirements for his people. The law pointed to Christ and his new spiritual kingdom. Now Christ has come, the need for keeping ceremonial law is over...

Circumcision (v 21) possibly indicated that sin needed to be "cut away" for a child to be part of the Lord's family of Israel. Jesus had no sin, but he came to remove the sins of others. Believers today have been circumcised, not literally, but by God's Spirit, in their hearts. By God's grace, we have been set apart from our sin and have that mark of belonging to the Lord's family.

Purification (v 22, 24) took place after 40 days. All that time had to pass before a woman who had given birth could once again worship God in the temple. Until then, her discharges made her ceremonially unclean. For purification there must be sacrifice (v 24). For Mary, the text makes clear that this was the poor person's offering of two doves.

Dedication (v 23) to the Lord was expected, but the child could be redeemed by payment. Yes, the Redeemer was "redeemed"! Redemption money (5 shekels) must be paid for the firstborn son, instead of giving the child to the Lord's service (for he belonged to the Lord by right). This pointed to the redemption price that Jesus paid later to purchase his people. Christians have been redeemed at the price of Jesus' blood. And so we belong to the Lord as his son or daughter!

Do we sufficiently grasp the importance of purity before a holy God? The Old Testament laws were so particular about uncleanness—and purification was a long and costly process. Praise God that Jesus came to completely wash away sin; in Jesus, believers are pure and blameless.

✔ Apply

The "law of the Lord" for Christians to follow is the law of love; Christ has fulfilled the demands of the law for us, so we may freely serve him and follow his ways.

❓ *Are you showing your gratitude? What opportunities will the next 72 hours give you to do so?*

A song for Christmas

Happy Christmas! Have a great day, and know something of the joy of the Christmas gospel. You probably have a full day ahead (or behind) so enjoy this song of joy.

Truly spiritual

Read Luke 2:25-27

- ❓ *What kind of man is Simeon?*
- ❓ *What do you think it means that Jesus would be the "consolation" of Israel?*

Simeon, like many godly Jews, had been longing to see the Messiah, who would bring consolation to Israel (see Isaiah 40:1-2)—that is, comfort and guidance. Unlike others, Simeon knew that he would see him. Here was a man of God. His whole life was focused on living right and waiting patiently. Even before the age of the Spirit, Simeon was blessed with the Holy Spirit in his life. Imagine Simeon's immense joy to discover his Saviour in the temple!

Truly remarkable

Read Luke 2:28-33

- ❓ *What is truly remarkable about Simeon's song of praise?*

A stunning insight that left his parents astonished. While others found it hard to come to terms with Old Testament prophecies promising that the Messiah would bless the despised Gentiles, they were a delight to Simeon, a matter for praise and wonder.

Not surprisingly, Joseph and Mary were amazed. But there were more truths to come that would make them think long and hard about this child...

A piercing sword

Read Luke 2:34-35

- ❓ *What does Simeon mean by these cryptic statements?*
- ❓ *How would Mary have responded to them, do you think?*

Some of the phrases are hard to understand, but the drift is clear. Simeon was already looking beyond the glory of the gift of Jesus, the Saviour—he could begin to see the pain and sorrow Jesus would suffer, the division and the heart-searching he would bring, the grief his death would mean for Mary.

⌄ Apply

Could Simeon see, by faith, the reason for all this? Could he see salvation by the death of Jesus on the cross? We cannot tell. But this much is sure: Simeon had seen enough to be ready to "rest in peace"—to rest in Jesus as his Saviour—even as the child rested in his arms.

- ❓ *Have you seen enough in Jesus to know that death can now be embraced with joy, rather than feared?*

⌃ Pray

Give thanks that today you celebrate a light of revelation to the whole world. Pray that the light of Jesus would illuminate all that happens today.

Prayerful prophetess

Always busy at the church... often up at night praying... spends whole days fasting... This sounds like a description of an energetic young Christian, but is in fact an 84-year old!

All out for God
Read Luke 2:36-38

❓ *Why is there so much detail about Anna's life and family, do you think?*

❓ *What do we learn about her character and priorities?*

❓ *Having seen Jesus, what does she do?*

Exactly how old Anna was is debated. The point is that she was very old, but very devoted; still full of commitment to God.

Paul encourages us to "pray continually" (1 Thessalonians 5:17). Anna seems almost literally to have done that, from the description in Luke 2:37. Maybe she had a room within the temple complex, or perhaps it is just a figurative way to describe her regularity ("she's always there!"). Either way, Anna devoted a great deal of time to prayer.

🔽 Apply

If you are still young, don't you find Anna's example a great challenge? You have far more energy—but how much of it is directed towards serving God?

If you are older, what an encouragement to think that, however weak you may be, prayer is counted as serving God.

Answered prayer
Read Luke 2:38 again

❓ *What do you think is meant by the phrase "redemption of Jerusalem"?*

Prayer is not just a holy way of spending time. God had answered Anna's pleading for God to come and visit his people, to revive them, to send the Messiah to save them. There were just a few who were still looking and praying for the "redemption of Jerusalem"—now she could see the Redeemer with her own eyes.

🔼 Pray

"But we have our jobs to do, school to go to, family to care for. We can't always be praying as Anna did..."

True. But we can do everything in a prayerful attitude. We can keep our thoughts shooting up to God, conscious of his presence, relying on his help, thanking him for his goodness. And when we have to wait for something, or when our mind does not need to be occupied, we can talk to the Lord about the things on our hearts—but more importantly, the things we know are on *his* heart.

NAHUM: Severe comfort

When was the last time you were surprised or challenged by God's character? Nahum is a quick burst of a book—but it punches well beyond its size!

The bringer of comfort

Read Nahum 1:1

❓ *What is Nahum's book about?*

❓ *Do you recall anything else in the Bible about this city?*

Nahum is set around 664-612 BC. Nineveh was the capital city of Assyria, a vast and powerful nation with a brutal reputation. In 722 BC Assyria had conquered and exiled the northern kingdom of Israel, a divinely-ordained punishment for Israel's rebellion against God. As we read on, we'll see that Nahum is particularly writing for the remaining tribes of Israel, known as the southern kingdom of Judah. We know virtually nothing about Nahum, but his name and title is key to the whole book. Nahum means "comfort"—and while Elkoshite was probably a reference to where he lived, it also can be translated as "God of Discomfort/Severity".

Who is the LORD?

Read Nahum 1:2-3a

❓ *What's your instinctive reaction when you see God described as "jealous" or "taking vengeance" (v 2)?*

❓ *How would these verses be a source of "uncomfortable comfort"?*

As one of the Bible's defining descriptions of the LORD's character, these verses echo Exodus 34:6-7, which are referenced through-out the Scriptures. Fascinatingly, they'd also been used in reference to Nineveh a century earlier. The prophet Jonah had been out-raged—though apparently unsurprised—by God's grace towards the Assyrian capital af-ter their city-wide repentance (Jonah 4:1-2). In a sense, Nahum is the sequel to Jonah, but now we find that Assyria has returned to its greedy and blood-thirsty ways...

The God of de-creation

Read Nahum 1:3b-6

❓ *Take a moment to imagine each action listed. What kind of a God is this?*

The place of comfort

Read Nahum 1:7-8

❓ *Given what we've read so far in Nahum, what's your reaction to verse 7?*

❓ *How are these verses beginning to flesh out Nahum's message of comfort?*

One writer has defined God's jealousy as "a strong desire to maintain relational faithful-ness that belongs to you".

❓ *Given this definition, why might God's jealousy be a precious thing?*

⌃ Pray

Ask God to reveal himself to you through Nahum, and that you would know his mer-cy and comfort are real.

Behold your God

Life can be hard as a follower of God. Thankfully, Nahum is not naive about the different forces at work in this world which oppose God's rule and God's people.

But Nahum is also confident about where true and lasting comfort is found...

Rediscovering the LORD
Read Nahum 1:9-11

- ❓ *What is Nineveh's fate (v 9-10)?*
- ❓ *What does the imagery of twisted thorns, drunkenness and easily-flammable stubble (v 10) convey about Assyria?*
- ❓ *How does verse 11 give clarity to what Assyria was doing?*

There is a strong argument for translating verse 9 as "What do you think concerning the LORD?" It seems Nahum isn't just declaring that Assyria has underestimated God. It's also his mission to demonstrate to God's people that they can find great comfort in his nature. While Assyria "plots evil against the LORD' (v 11), Judah's hope is to be found in remembering just who God is. This is the LORD, who will defend his people and keep his promises.

Reversing the sentence
Read Nahum 1:12-14

- ❓ *What does verse 12 tell us about Assyria's strength at the time of writing?*
- ❓ *As in verse 9, Nahum addresses God's people in verses 12-13. What is God's promise?*
- ❓ *How does verse 14 provide an all-encompassing judgment on Assyria?*

Rejoicing in victory
Read Nahum 1:15

- ❓ *Why does Judah have reason to be glad?*
- ❓ *How does Nahum call Judah to respond? Why might these things be especially listed?*
- ❓ *Given that Assyria was undefeated, do you think it would have been easy for Judah to believe Nahum's message?*

TIME OUT

The apostle Paul alludes to verse 15 in Romans 10:15, describing the importance of people proclaiming the message of Christ. Of course, a messenger had a crucial function in making events known in Nahum's day. But imagine the moment when you first spot in the distance the messenger making his way to your camp—and now imagine the feeling when it becomes evident he has good news on his lips.

☑ Apply

In time we will consider how God opposes those who oppress his people. But for today, behold your God! See his commitment to his people and promises—seen ultimately in Jesus' victory on the cross. Neither sin, the world nor the devil can stand in his way. Ultimately it is Christ who proclaims "peace" to us—"to you who were far away... and to those who were near" (Ephesians 2:17).

All bets are off

Do you ever read horrific stories of Christians being persecuted, or think of your own situation, and wish that God would do more to protect his people?

Lights, camera, attack!
Read Nahum 2:1-6

> ❓ *What is the tone of verse 1?*
> ❓ *How does verse 2 set Nineveh's destruction within a bigger purpose?*

"Jacob" was a common term for God's people, and Nahum may be paralleling the promise of Judah's restored splendour with the life-story of Abraham's grandson, the original Jacob. Though once shamed (deceiving his brother, Esau, to steal his father's blessing), his life ended in splendour, mourned even by Pharaoh's servants (Genesis 50).

> ❓ *How does the vivid imagery of Nahum 2:3-6 make you feel?*

These verses are like cinematic slow-motion sequences: the colossal onslaught, the hopeless defence, the desperate devastation. It's incredible to remember this evocative description had not yet occurred. God's people were being comforted with a vision of the future they couldn't yet see.

The script is written
Read Nahum 2:7-10

> ❓ *How certain are these events (v 7a)?*
> ❓ *What will happen to Nineveh—and why is this particularly ironic?*

Like water disappearing into soil, Assyria's future is irreversible. But it's also a reversal of the crimes she has committed: the wealth she had amassed is now amassed by others; the body-shaking fear she caused is now felt by her own citizens.

Tables turned
Read Nahum 2:11-13

> ❓ *Why is a lion a particularly good image for Assyria (v 12)?*
> ❓ *What happens to this "lion" (v 11, 13)?*
> ❓ *God exposes the dark underbelly of Assyria's successes (v 12). Why is this important?*

While often associated with regal finesse, lions are brutal and blood-thirsty predators. This was Assyria, ruthlessly devouring cities full of people made in the image of God.

✅ Apply

While we were once all enemies of God (Romans 5:6-11; John 3:36; Colossians 1:21), this passage is an assurance that, just as Nineveh was overthrown, so God will defeat those who persist in opposing his people.

God is not deaf to the cries of his people around the world. Neither is he threatened by the seeming power of those who persecute his people. Nahum's message shows us that God's patience is not to be confused for his powerlessness. He will act to save and judge.

Brought to justice

How much does it matter to you that God is a God of justice? And how much have we considered what this means in a world ravaged by evil?

Just deserts
Read Nahum 3:1

"Woe" was often used to introduce a devastating threat. Often associated with mourning the dead, it underlined bad things were on their way to those who deserved them.

> ❓ *How does this verse underline the cause of Nineveh's fate?*

The vast might and wealth of the Assyrians had not been accumulated simply by a few good trade deals. They were experts in plunder, deception and blood-thirsty pillaging.

⌄ Apply

As a Christian, do you ever find yourself moved by injustice, oppression and falsehood? Sometimes we can simply feel overwhelmed by what's wrong with our world, but at other times we can struggle to look beyond our own horizons. Maybe we could even be accused of being blind to injustice or abuse that occur seemingly "on our doorstep".

> ❓ *How often do you think about God's feelings towards the evil all around us? Do you ever consider his attitude towards racism, or human trafficking, or abortion, or sexual grooming?*

Nahum's stark verdict of God's judgment upon Assyria is a reminder of our Lord's severe and holy hatred of evil.

Enslaved
Read Nahum 3:2-4

> ❓ *How does Nahum develop the graphic battle imagery of 2:3-10?*
> ❓ *According to 3:4, what are Assyria's offences?*
> ❓ *Why do you think Nahum chooses the metaphor of verse 4?*

Shamed
Read Nahum 3:5-7

> ❓ *How does Nahum now develop the imagery of verse 4?*
> ❓ *What is this metaphor saying that the LORD will ultimately do to Assyria?*

These are uncomfortable verses to imagine. Assyria has become a spectacle, shamed before a watching world. Nahum's "comfort" to God's people is that Assyria is comfortless (v 7).

⌃ Pray

Can you imagine hearing verse 5 said against you? It's a terrifying prospect. Yet Nahum's shocking imagery takes us beyond the ruins of Nineveh to Golgotha. Stripped of his clothes and hanging from a Roman execution device, Jesus became a spectacle to the world. He faced the judgment of God, being stricken, cursed, and made "to be sin for us" (2 Corinthians 5:21). *Praise him now!*

Fait accompli

This brief but powerful book is a wake-up call to the reality of God's justice and righteousness—even when we feel we are forgotten or his reputation abandoned.

Look around you
Read Nahum 3:8-11

❷ *What seems to have occurred to the Egyptian city of Thebes?*
❷ *What does Nahum emphasise about Thebes?*
❷ *What should Assyria be learning from Nahum's lesson in current affairs?*

Thebes had fallen to Assyria in 663 BC, helping us date Nahum to after that point. Despite being protected by the Nile (v 8) and having alliances with powerful nations like Ethiopia ("Cush") and Egypt (v 9), she was still brutally raided.

Try as you might
Read Nahum 3:12-17

❷ *How does the imagery of verse 12 demonstrate both Assyria's apparent flourishing and its vulnerability?*
❷ *Of what prospect are verses 14-15 warning Assyria of?*
❷ *What does Nahum's comparison in verses 16-17 highlight?*

A word to the king
Read Nahum 3:18-19

❷ *Who are these final verses in Nahum addressed to?*
❷ *Why would verse 18 be a terrifying prospect for any monarch?*

❷ *How does the imagery of a fatal wound underline Assyria's future?*

Strikingly, the final words of Nahum don't focus in on Assyria's demise but on how others will respond to it.

❷ *Why do you think Nahum ends with this emphasis? What does it highlight about the reason for Nineveh's suffering?*

The applause of verse 19 is not "gleeful gloating" but a sincere celebration of God's vindication as he is seen to keep his promises to his people. God's revealed character (1:3) will be demonstrated in time and history, giving Nineveh a "fatal wound" (3:19). As Nahum promises, Nineveh was wiped off the face of the earth by the Babylonian-Medan alliance in 612 BC and truly became a "hidden city" (2:11). It was only when archaeologists discovered its remains in 1842, near Mosul, Iraq, that its existence was finally proved.

⌄ Apply

Do you remember how "Nahum the Elkoshite" (1:1) could be translated "Comfort from the Uncomfortable God"?

❷ *How will Nahum's vision of a comforting uncomfortable God shape your view of life in the coming year?*
❷ *How does the assurance of the Lord's faithfulness bring you comfort amid injustice and hardship, and hope for the year ahead?*

Introduce a friend to

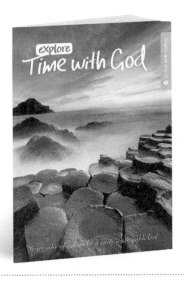

explore

If you're enjoying using *Explore*, why not introduce a friend? *Time with God* is our introduction to daily Bible reading and is a great way to get started with a regular time with God. It includes 28 daily readings along with articles, advice and practical tips on how to apply what the passage teaches.

Why not order a copy for someone you would like to encourage?

Coming up next...

❤ Hebrews
with Frank Price

❤ Romans 1 – 8
with Tim Chester

❤ Easter from Genesis
with Paul Jump and Anna Marsh

❤ Proverbs
with Martin Davy

 Don't miss your copy. Contact your local Christian bookshop or church agent, or visit:

UK & Europe: thegoodbook.co.uk
info@thegoodbook.co.uk
Tel: 0333 123 0880

North America: thegoodbook.com
info@thegoodbook.com
Tel: 866 244 2165

Australia: thegoodbook.com.au
info@thegoodbook.com.au
Tel: (02) 9564 3555

New Zealand: thegoodbook.co.nz
info@thegoodbook.co.nz
Tel: (+64) 3 343 2463

Join the *explore* community

The *Explore* Facebook group is a community of people who use *Explore* to study the Bible each day.

This is the place to share your thoughts, questions, encouragements and prayers as you read *Explore*, and interact with other readers, as well as contributors, from around the world. No questions are too simple or too difficult to ask.

JOIN NOW:
www.facebook.com/groups/tgbc.explore